PLYMOUTH CATHEDRAL
The story of a people
1858 ~ 2008

Celebrating 150 years

PLYMOUTH CATHEDRAL
The story of a people
1858 ~ 2008

Published by
The Dean & Chapter of
Plymouth Cathedral
Cathedral House, Cecil Street,
Plymouth PL1 5HW.

© Martin Dunning 2008

The right of Martin Dunning to be identified
as the author of this work has been asserted in accordance
with Sections 77 & 78 of the
Copyright Designs and Patents Act 1988.

A CIP catalogue record of this book is available from
The British Library.
ISBN 978-0-9559984-0-9

All rights reserved. No part of this publication may
be reproduced, stored in a retrieval system, or
transmitted in any form or by any means,
electronic, mechanical, photocopying, recording or otherwise
without the prior permission of the publishers.

Typeset in 10/11pt Baskerville, edited and produced
by Adrian Wardle. Researched by Tom Healy.
Printed by Latimer Trend & Co Ltd, Plymouth: www.trends.co.uk

Proceeds from the sale of this book will be used for the general purposes
of the Cathedral of St Mary & St Boniface, Plymouth, Devon, UK
which is part of the Roman Catholic Diocese of Plymouth.

Registered Charity No. 213227.

Plymouth Cathedral

The story of a people

1858 ~ 2008

by Martin Dunning

ACKNOWLEDGEMENTS

The author wishes to thank
Canon Bartholomew Nannery, BA
Dean of Plymouth Cathedral
for his inspiration and advice
together with the Abbot of Downside, the Rt Rev
Dom Aidan Bellenger, OSB, MA, PhD, FSA, FRHistS, FRSA
for his kind and expert help with this book.

Thanks also to Fr Michel Kirkpatrick, BA (Div)
of Plymouth Cathedral as well as researcher Tom Healy, BA
and Adrian Wardle, editor.

Many thanks to the past and present
parishioners of the Cathedral
for their reminiscences and photographs
which have formed a significant part of this work.

Contemporary photography by Alistair Davis
Tel. 01752 895576.

The Bishop of Plymouth.

Foreword

THE CATHEDRAL CHURCH of St Mary and St Boniface symbolises everything we hold most precious about the faith that we profess and try to live. It is a building that must persuade us to be forever grateful to those who went before us, and handed down to us the faith of our fathers over 2000 years. Our debt of gratitude will always be immense.

It is a building that will challenge us in the present to come to an understanding of our faith that will enable us to give an account of what we believe and hope to anyone who inquires. Look around at the foundational symbols of our faith, Baptism, Forgiveness of sin, the Eucharist, the Word of God, the presence of the Bishop and his Clergy, the People of God itself, Our Lady and the Saints. They all say to us that the Lord is alive and well and wants us to be his hands and feet. Perhaps the Chapel of Saints George and Patrick now dedicated to Justice and Peace needs to be prominent in our understanding and living of our faith.

We leave what we belong to, to those coming after us. As we have been blessed by receiving these gifts from the Lord, so we share that blessing with those who come after us. The details of the mission agenda of faith may be different in the future but we need to leave behind everything that the Lord has revealed to us about Himself and us, so that the new mission may be pursued.

This cathedral is a symbol of our faith. We need to live that faith in such a way that others may wish to know of the Lord Jesus Christ.

In fide,

✝Christopher **Bishop of Plymouth**

Rt Rev Christopher Budd, Bishop of Plymouth.

The Cathedral Dean.

Introduction

IT IS A PLEASURE to greet you as you start to read about Plymouth Cathedral in this, our 150th year. You will discover that the cathedral has undergone many changes over the years at the hands of my predecessors.

Rev Canon Bartholomew Nannery, Dean of Plymouth Cathedral.

In more recent times, I myself have had the privilege of being part of the re-ordering of this wonderful building to reflect not only the changes wrought by the Second Vatican Council but also to fulfil the vision of our Bishop to make all our worship and liturgy more inclusive and less remote and distant from the people.

And to be true, it is the people rather than the buildings who are the the Church in Plymouth. In fact, The Holy Father, Pope Benedict XVI, in imparting his Apostolic Blessing to us for this historic anniversary, reminds the people that 'they themselves are God's temple, the dwelling place of the Holy Spirit.' (cf. 1 Cor 3:16).

As you read these pages, you will discover that it isn't just the clergy who have selflessly ministered to the people of Plymouth over the years. There are also the religious communities of men and women, teachers, catechists, parish committees and countless individual churchgoers. It is they who, in times of pestilence, poverty, war and peace, have taken the love, compassion and succour of Jesus Christ from the pews into the homes and hearts of the people of this delightful city by the sea.

So is this the story of a cathedral? Not quite. It is the story of a people ... inspired and fortified by the Word of God.

Canon Bartholomew Nannery,
Dean of Plymouth Cathedral

Restoration of the Hierarchy
PART I ~ *The first 50 years.*

THE FIRST 50 YEARS

Chapter One

25TH MARCH 1858: the last bars of the *Te Deum* echoed around the pillars of Bath stone, the granite floor and the high altar of Plymouth marble. Plymouth's Roman Catholic Cathedral of St Mary and St Boniface was finally open, evidence in stone and mortar both of God's love and how much the religious climate had changed for the better over the past three centuries.

1858: The first photograph of Plymouth's Roman Catholic cathedral. There are cattle grazing in the fields where Notre Dame School was to be built. The spire was added later.

Following Henry VIII's break with the Roman Catholic Church and the subsequent Dissolution of the Monasteries, his successors had, for the most part, maintained a strict Protestant regime. During the reign of Elizabeth I, the ever present threat of invasion by Spain had hardened anti-Catholic feeling, especially in a front line town such as Plymouth, where men such as Drake, Hawkins and Grenville grew rich and famous by repeatedly thwarting the Spanish. Perhaps inevitably this left a deep suspicion of all things Catholic in the minds of Plymouth folk who, it would seem, leaned naturally towards the Church of England. Indeed, in 1641 a group of Puritan merchants, perceiving the parish church of St Andrew to be too 'Catholic', began building the rival Charles Church. Ironically, permission for this came from Charles I, whose Catholic leanings were in part responsible for the outbreak of the Civil War in 1642. In that war, Plymouth took the Parliamentarian side and was besieged by the Royalists under Prince Maurice in 1643, culminating in the Sabbath Day Fight in which the Roundhead garrison, supported by townsfolk, finally routed

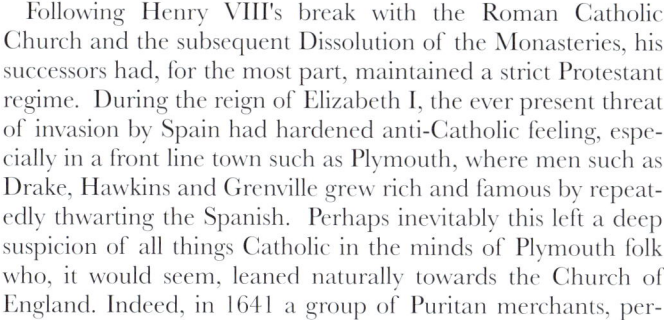

LEFT: Prince Maurice, nephew of King Charles I, by Nathaniel Thache.
(Royal Collection)

PLYMOUTH CATHEDRAL 1858-2008   1

THE FIRST 50 YEARS   *Restoration of the Hierarchy*

the Cavalier army. This keen defence of Parliamentarian values suggests that Plymouth did not provide fertile ground for the faithful.

There was a respite for the faithful during the reign of James II, Britain's last Catholic monarch. James established the four Vicars Apostolic, missionary bishops responsible to Rome, who presided over the whole of the Catholic Church in England and Wales, and in 1687, the king appointed Christopher Turner as chaplain to the soldiery of the Citadel. Turner is known to have performed one baptism, that of "Flin, Joseph son of James of Ireland." The respite was brief, however, and when William of Orange deposed James in 1688, the Protestant repression of Catholics meant that there are no records of any Catholicism in Plymouth for almost a century. Outside Plymouth, families such as the Carys at Torre and the Cliffords of Chudleigh, wealthy enough to pay the fines, maintained priests and discreetly supported the local Catholic community. Exeter seems to have had a Catholic community in the town, albeit one that functioned intermittently, but on the Plymouth community there was silence until 1767, when the Bishop of Exeter drew up a List of Papists for the government. The list contains twelve names for the parish of St Andrew and a lonely David Herbert for that of St Charles. Priests did visit to say Mass from time to time, one of them being Edward Williams, chaplain to the Chester family near Kingsbridge. In 1772 he wrote that "I had carried on business in Plymouth upwards of 20 years, being the first who undertook anything of that kind in the memory of any man."

PLYMTON DEANERY

Papists	Age	Occupation	Resident
PLYMOUTH			
St. Andrew			
Eleanor Brooking, wife of	c.40		c.20y
Joseph Brooking, malster			
Michael Fanning	34	merchant	9y
Mary Fanning, his sister	21	do.	
Elizabeth Fanning, his brother's widow	30		5y
James Herring	50	boatman	27y
Winifred Herring his wife	40		13y
Margaret Herring his daughter	14		10y
Joanna Herring, his daughter	9		9y
John Larking	26	Clerk to Mr. Fanning	7y
George Mark	50	victualler	3½y
John Murphy	50	boatman	18y
Catharine, his wife	42	do.	
M 5			
F 7			
12			
St. Charles			
David Herbert	c.60	innkeeper	
M 1			
1			

1767: The Bishop of Exeter's List of Papists.

By the late 18th century, then, the Catholic Church in England and Wales was operating without a proper structure and was, essentially, still a missionary church, without cathedrals, churches and even parish priests. The Industrial Revolution was getting into its stride, slums were growing, and the missioners struggled on in the face of ever growing demands.

One of the areas of growth was Plymouth, where the seemingly endless wars with France had prompted the Admiralty to undertake the construction of a new dockyard to support the Western Fleet. The development of Plymouth Dock (known at

Restoration of the Hierarchy

THE FIRST 50 YEARS

the time merely as Dock, and now Devonport) resulted in the influx of a large Irish Catholic workforce, a fact that did not go unnoticed by Bishop Walmesley, the Vicar Apostolic of the Western District. In 1782 Walmesley appointed the newly ordained Charles Timmings to minister to the Catholics of Dartmouth, Totnes, and Plymouth. Timmings reported that in Plymouth " ...the congregation ... is between 40 and 50, almost all Irish and chiefly living at the Dock, working men or keeping Public Houses." Discouraged by the difficulty of spreading himself so thinly, and quite pos-

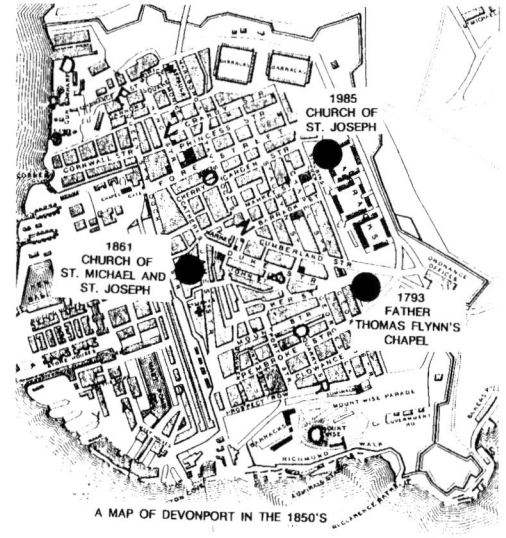

A MAP OF DEVONPORT IN THE 1850'S

sibly by the premises in Plymouth, which the Bishop himself described as "a most miserable wretched chapel in a horrible garret", Timmings, after a short sojourn in Plymouth, eventually returned to Dartmouth and Bishop Walmesley appointed Thomas Flynn to serve the Catholic flock of the ever-growing Dock.

1793: The location of Father Thomas Flynn's first chapel above a stable to serve the growing Catholic population of Plymouth Dock, now Devonport.

Flynn, a Franciscan born in Ireland, arrived in 1793 and threw himself into his mission, establishing a chapel above (appropriately) a stable at the back of the George Inn at Devonport. He immediately started seeking out his flock, many of whom, not having seen a priest in years, might have been feeling a little despondent. Flynn's registers open with the marriage of Lawrence Carney and Margaret Clifford on 20th November, and continue with other marriages and baptisms. A look at the names in the registers is revealing; at first, most are Irish, with just a smattering of English, and as time passes foreign names begin to appear, the result of exiles from the Napoleonic War.

A contemporary describes Flynn as being "a man of zeal and herculean strength", and no doubt these qualities stood him in good stead in the rough and ready atmosphere of a naval town on a war footing. Occasionally, national events would have tested him: in 1797 the Spithead Mutiny broke out, the result of poor pay, worse conditions, and brutal discipline. Sailors in

THE FIRST 50 YEARS

Restoration of the Hierarchy

Devonport, smarting from the hanging from the yardarm of six Irish sailors, came out in sympathy and the red flag of revolution was flown from every ship. The ringleaders – three men by the names of Lee, Coffee and Braning, were summarily tried and sentenced to be publicly executed on the Hoe. Two clergymen were on hand: the Reverend Robert Hawker attended Lee and "a priest of the Church of Rome" his co-conspirators.

1807: Abbé Guilbert records the blessing of the Chapel of St Mary's.

History does not record the name of the Catholic priest, but it is logical to assume that it was Flynn. He and Hawker knelt in prayer with the doomed men and then left, weeping, as the firing squad loaded their muskets.

Time took its toll of Flynn and after ten years he left for America. His successor was Abbé Louis Guilbert who, on 20th December 1807, opened the Chapel of St Mary's and St John the Evangelist on St Mary Street in Stonehouse. This, the first proper Catholic church in Plymouth, was a vast improvement on the grubby chapel above the stable in Dock, stood near the entrance of the imposing Royal Naval Hospital (now Millfields) and at the edge of Mill Pool Marshes. The site was bought with the help of Rowland Conyers, a benefactor who had set up a trust to provide support for Catholic mariners in Dartmouth, Falmouth and Plymouth. The tidal marshes flooded the surrounding area: what are now Clarence Place, Manor Street and King Street were often inundated, and with Stonehouse Creek then running up to Pennycomequick the chapel would have appeared, on a high spring tide, to be occupying an island. Attached to St Mary's were buildings occupied by the Sisters of Notre Dame de Namur and later the Little Sisters of the Poor. The Sisters would have spent plenty of time at the Royal Naval Hospital

The old St Mary's in Stonehouse.

1858-2008 PLYMOUTH CATHEDRAL

Restoration of the Hierarchy
THE FIRST 50 YEARS

ministering to the needs of the patients – thousands of marines and sailors, sick and wounded, who were brought up Stonehouse Creek and disembarked at the hospital's Jetty Gate.

At the time of the chapel's construction the area was quite rural, but as the century progressed, the land from Stonehouse Bridge to Manor Street became built up with thousands of houses occupied by dockyard workers, an increasing number of whom were Irish. A majority of priests too were Irish, and it was one of their number, Father Henry Riley, who extended St Mary's Chapel, adding sacristies and a sanctuary and a gallery over the west end.

A look at the list of the names of parish priests of St Mary's reveals something of the circumstances of the time: four have Irish names and three French, indicating that the Church was still having to "import" priests, as it were, and that the recruitment of English priests was in a minority. This is a reflection of a larger picture of immigration from Ireland. Driven by poverty in their native land, a constant stream of men and women crossed the Irish Sea, heading for the big emigré communities of Liverpool, London and Manchester and jobs in shipping, the railways, and industry. A smaller number spread out over the country and in particular to Naval and garrison towns such as Aldershot, Portsmouth – and Plymouth. By 1840 the Irish population in England and Wales was 290,000, a figure that was almost to double as a result of the potato famine of 1845-47, with the effect that in the mid-19th century the Church in England and Wales consisted chiefly of Irish immigrants. Privations abounded, and not just for the Irish. In 1850 cholera laid its dread hand on Plymouth, and raged in particular through the squalid, rat-infested mazes of Stonehouse. One tenth of Plymouth's population fell prey to the disease and 900 died. Thomas McDonnel, priest of St Mary's, showed great courage in ministering to the sick and dying, ably backed up by the Little Sisters of the Poor. Three years earlier, in Liverpool, 15,000 died from typhus, including ten priests, and in Newcastle Bishop Riddell, Vicar Apostolic of the Northern District, died of the same disease while ministering to the sick. These were trying times, both spiritually and temporally.

It was against this background that things at last began to change for the hard-pressed holders of the faith. The Catholic Emancipation Act of 1829 reflected a general relaxing of the attitude towards Catholicism, and

In 1850 cholera laid its dread hand on Plymouth, and raged in particular through the squalid, rat-infested mazes of Stonehouse.

Pius IX whose Apostolic Letter of 29 September 1850 restored the Catholic Hierarchy.

PLYMOUTH CATHEDRAL 1858-2008

THE FIRST 50 YEARS

Restoration of the Hierarchy

THE THIN END OF THE WEDGE.
DARING ATTEMPT TO BREAK INTO A CHURCH.

1850: A Punch cartoon showing Cardinal Wiseman and Pope Pius IX, reflecting the mood of the establishment at the time. (Punch Ltd)

the climate was a far cry from the suspicion and repression of the late 17th and early 18th centuries.

In 1840 Pope Gregory XVI divided England into eight Vicariates. The new Western District comprised Somerset, Gloucester, Wiltshire, Cornwall, Devon and Dorset; its new leader, Bishop Baines, had a mere 40 priests and 18,000 Catholics. This shot in the arm for English Catholicism proved but a transitional phase, however, for on 29th September 1850 Pope Pius IX announced the Restoration of the English Hierarchy under Cardinal Nicholas Wiseman as Archbishop of Westminster.

Wiseman, on his elevation to Cardinal, wrote his first Pastoral, in which he stated that he would "govern and shall continue to govern, the counties of Middlesex, Hertford, and Essex as ordinary thereof, and those of Surrey, Sussex, Kent, Berkshire and Hampshire, with the islands annexed, as administrator with ordinary jurisdiction." The papers weren't impressed, with *The Times* thundering that "we confess that we can only regard it as one of the grossest acts of folly and impertinence which the court of Rome has venture to commit since the crown and people of England threw off its yoke." Queen Victoria wasn't amused: "Am I Queen of England, or am I not?" There were protests all over the country, and on Guy Fawkes night that year effigies of Pius IX were burned.

Archbishop Wiseman's incautious use of language had touched a nerve, revealing the anti-Catholic undercurrents beneath the apparently tolerant surface of English society. He sought to neutralise the venom in the measured words of an "Appeal to the English People", in which he identified the arena of the Catholic Mission in terms not of politics, but in the "labyrinths of lanes and courts, and alleys and slums, nests of ignorance, vice, depravity, and crime, as well as of squalor, wretchedness and disease; whose atmosphere is typhus, whose ventilation is cholera; in which swarms a huge and almost countless population, in great measure, at least, Catholic; haunts of filth, which no sewage committee can reach, dark corners, which no lighting can brighten."

Restoration of the Hierarchy

THE FIRST 50 YEARS

Today, we would call it a mission statement.

Away from the rhetoric there were administrative matters to capture the new Cardinal's attention. If the Restoration of the English Hierarchy was to mean anything, it must rise to the pastoral challenge presented by poverty, sickness, lack of sanitation and a dearth of spiritual sustenance. To this end, twelve new dioceses were created, including that of Plymouth, following the law at the time that stated that no Catholic diocese should have the same name as a Church of England one. The Diocese of Plymouth stretched from Poole in the east to Land's End in the west, and from England's most southerly point at the Lizard to the wild shore of Exmoor in the north, and taking in the counties of Cornwall, Devon and Dorset. This new, smaller entity was easier to administer and meant that the new bishop would not have to dilute his efforts over the vast area of the old District. That said, the new diocese was long and narrow and far from the big cities, communications were poor, and its Catholic population was dispersed over a huge area.

Bishop George Errington, first Bishop of Plymouth, 1851-1855.

The man given the task of bringing this embryonic diocese to life was Doctor George Errington, the first Bishop of Plymouth. A Yorkshireman who had at one time been Vice-Rector to Wiseman at the English College in Rome, at the time of his appointment he was priest at St John's in Salford, where Cardinal Wiseman consecrated him Bishop on 25th July 1851. On his arrival in Plymouth the new bishop must have been dismayed to find that there was not enough room for him to reside at St Mary's. Edmund Bastard of Kitley House put up Bishop Errington temporarily, and when Thomas McDonnell took over a mission in Somerset that October, the bishop was finally able to move into Stonehouse, where "by his affability, learning and unobtrusive ways, he soon overcame the recent burst of bigotry excited by the recent establishment of the Catholic Hierarchy." The handbook of the Fourth National Catholic Congress in 1913, describes him thus: "He had a wonderful physique and great powers of endurance. Duty was almost the only thought which occupied his resolute and unbending mind. Very hard and Spartan in his ways, some were frightened by him from a

Twelve new dioceses were created, including Plymouth.

THE FIRST 50 YEARS   *Restoration of the Hierarchy*

false impression often created unwillingly by such men. For he was a man really of a very tender heart, a great lover of the poor and of the discredited."

Home of the Lords Clifford of Chudleigh for over 400 years, Ugbrooke House is a Robert Adam castellated manor house with a Capability Brown park and a 17th century Catholic chapel redesigned by Adam. (www.ugbrooke.co.uk)

Bishop Errington's endurance and resolution were characteristics that served him well. As well as inaugurating the Cathedral Chapter in 1853 and holding a Synod at Ugbrooke Park in 1854, he had all the usual duties of administering the sacraments, supporting his priests, visiting the sick, and pushing forward the Stonehouse mission. The appointment in 1852 of William Clifford as priest of the mission must have lightened his burden, but Bishop Errington's workload was still enough to make a strong man blanch. Merely travelling around the Diocese would have been demanding; the railway had arrived in Plymouth in 1848, but there it ended, and trips such as the Bishop's weekly visit to Dartmoor Prison, conducted in all weathers, would have involved long, gruelling coach journeys on appalling roads.

In 1855 Cardinal Wiseman raised Errington to the rank of Archbishop and summoned him to London to act as his coadjutor. Bishop Errington's later career was marked by controversy and a falling out with Wiseman, but his work in Plymouth had laid strong administrative and spiritual foundations, and now the stage was set for the entrance of the man who would build the city's first Catholic Cathedral, William Vaughan.

8   1858-2008 PLYMOUTH CATHEDRAL

Restoration of the Hierarchy   **THE FIRST 50 YEARS**

Canon Herbert Woollett

IF EVERY GREAT PERSON excels in his chosen domain, it often happens because he has at his back someone who can be relied upon to do the routine but necessary tasks and allow his superior to concentrate on the big issues.

Herbert Woollett was such a character. He arrived in Plymouth with Bishop Vaughan in 1855 to be the bishop's secretary and then parish priest of St Mary's, Stonehouse.

He moved into the still uncompleted Bishop's House in 1858 and became the first administrator of the cathedral in the same year. This task he was to perform for thirty years until his death in 1888 at the age of 71. In 1869 he was the author of that year's Advent Pastoral Letter, Bishop Vaughan being preoccupied in Rome at the First Vatican Council. This promulgated the doctrine of Papal Infallibility which the bishop supported but not, it appears, with any great enthusiasm. Canon Woollett was a man of many roles.

He became naval chaplain to HMS Hotspur, a hulk at anchor in the Tamar which the Admiralty provided as the church for Catholic sailors when it approved the provision of Catholic chaplains for the fleet.

He was to perform this role until 1887, the year before his death. Taken along with his other duties at the cathedral, he was Chairman of the Governors of the Cathedral School for much of his life, his must have been a career of unremitting toil. It probably weakened his health for, in his final years, he suffered from a serious heart condition.

Herbert Aubry Woollett was born in Monmouth in 1817. His family was one of those well-to-do families whose Catholicism was practised discreetly and who could afford to have him educated at one of those Catholic schools recently moved here from the continent. He received his education at Prior Park College, Bath. He was ordained by the Vicar Apostolic, Bishop Peter Baines in 1842 and moved to Lyme Regis as parish priest in what was still missionary territory. Within a few years he was in Plymouth where he was to remain for the rest of his life. He was made Doctor of Divinity in 1872.

He was a man of many parts, he founded the Secular Clergy Fund in 1861 in order to provide financial support for priests who had retired, and it was he whose efforts placed the fund on such a secure footing.

Herbert Woollett died in May 1888 after a series of heart attacks. He was buried in the Catholic section of Ford Park Cemetery and a granite tombstone marks his resting place. Apart from being the first administrator of the cathedral, he was the longest serving, none of his successors has served as long.   **Tom Healy**

THE FIRST 50 YEARS *Restoration of the Hierarchy*

The west end of Plymouth Cathedral with its new entrance and narthex.

Building the Cathedral — **THE FIRST 50 YEARS**

Chapter Two

WILLIAM VAUGHAN was born in Courtfield, Hereford in 1813 into a family that produced a remarkable number of bishops. By 1838 he was priest in charge of the Lyme Regis mission, and later took charge of the Clifton Pro-Cathedral of the Holy Apostles, where he was consecrated bishop on 16th September 1855 by Cardinal Wiseman. Bishop Vaughan seems to have made an impression on all who met him, as a description in marvellous, purple Edwardian prose from the handbook to the Fourth National Catholic Congress indicates:

"His career, completely screened from outside observation, was notoriously extraordinary to all who knew him. Most emphatically a ruler, his mind corresponded to his strikingly noble presence. Direct, simple in thought and speech, most slow in decision and swift in action he literally made the Diocese of Plymouth. As hinted, like most who have done much he has left no chronicles and his life cannot now be written, but the "Old Bishop" as he was affectionately called, will one day even have his legend. It was a delight to the people when he appeared in the pulpit. A thorough ecclesiastic, he had no thought beyond pushing forward the interests of Christ. In dealing with others his bluntness was often softened by a graciousness so very gracious that the fragrance of it remained for ever."

The task facing Bishop Vaughan on his arrival in Plymouth was immense. There were only 23 priests to cover the entire diocese, meaning that the average size of a mission was some 217 square miles, and within three years the number of priests was down to

Bishop William Vaughan. He was the nephew of Cardinal Thomas Weld of Lulworth in Dorset and the uncle of Cardinal Herbert Vaughan, the founder of Westminster Cathedral. LEFT: The Last Supper: detail from the Vaughan window in the south transept.

THE FIRST 50 YEARS Building the Cathedral

twelve. Not only was manpower in short supply, but money was tight, and there was still an outstanding debt of £500 on St Mary's Chapel. The clergy house in Stonehouse was too small to accommodate the new bishop, so, along with his Vicar General Canon Clifford and the priest in charge of St Mary's Dr McAuliffe, he rented a house at 2 Victoria Place. It was not a promising situation, and one that might have sapped the will of a lesser man, but Bishop Vaughan, who clearly believed 'where there's a will there's a way', had a vision and was determined to bring it to fruition.

The new bishop felt it vital that a cathedral was built to provide a spiritual focus for the diocese, while recognising more temporal needs in the shape of a new house for the clergy. Some would have advocated the more cautious approach of taking on only one project at a time, but not William Vaughan. Encouraged by the generosity of the people of the parish and of individual donors, on 20th February 1856 he was able to purchase a site in an area known as Fivefields, a meadow next to Ponteys Nursery. The cost, at one shilling and threepence a square foot, was £2,400, a sum that in 1856 was several year's pay for the average parishioner.

That Bishop Vaughan was able to buy the land was almost wholly down to Edmund Bastard, of Kitley, the man who, five years previously, had offered accommodation to Bishop Errington. Bastard offered £1,000 as a down payment on the cost of the site, and £250 a year to pay off the balance. The bishop launched an appeal for more funds and contracted the Bristol architects Joseph (later famous as the designer of the Hansom Cab) and Charles Hansom to draw the plans, which envisaged a simple but well-proportioned design in the early English Gothic style, able to seat about 700. A Stonehouse builder named Roberts put in a tender of £3,084 for the building of the cathedral, without the spire, which was to be added in 1867. A portion of the tower was raised in the initial construction, however, over the north entrance porch, to allow the placing of a bell. The tender was accepted on 22nd of May, the ground staked out, and work began in earnest on 10th June.

Kitley House near Plymouth. The former home of the Bastard family. (Kitley House Hotel)

Building the Cathedral **THE FIRST 50 YEARS**

Bishop Vaughan himself laid the foundation stone at the east end on 28th June.

Financially, the sudden death of Edmund Bastard and the consequent loss of some of his donation could have been a stumbling block, but providence intervened in the shape of one Miss Trelawney of Trelawne, who donated £3,000, and a friend of hers who offered £1,000, while a further £2,000 was raised in subscriptions by parishioners.

The cathedral walls, built from the handsome, pinky-grey Plymouth limestone that was at one time the staple building material of the city, rose steadily through the summer and autumn of 1856. In November, cracks appeared in some of the walls, but these were rectified and work continued; in January 1857 more cracks appeared, but these too were repaired and it seemed that the cathedral would be ready for its proposed consecration in August. By June, the roof was complete, but on 2nd June the contractor noticed some cracks in the south arch of the nave and sent a telegram to Charles Hansom in Bristol asking him to inspect the problem. Hansom arrived the following day and promptly set the workmen to shoring up the arches of the nave.

Unfortunately the Royal Navy unwittingly chose this crucial moment to intervene, as Bishop Graham later wrote: "during the morning Captain Jerringham of the 'Cambridge' gunnery ship began to practice some heavy new guns of a Turkish Man of War in the Sound; each explosion of which shook the unsteady work, and at length about one o'clock the brickwork suddenly subsided, bringing with it the entire roof of the nave and the south clerestory. No one however was injured for all had made a rapid retreat to the north porch except a carpenter, who escaped through the sacristy." Charles Hansom was dragged clear by one of the workmen in the nick of time. Rumours spread through the town to the effect that many had been killed and injured and on the following day morbid curiosity drew hundreds of sightseers, adding to the workload of the already hard-

A man-of war fires its guns.

THE FIRST 50 YEARS   Building the Cathedral

pressed building crew. Hansom drew up revised, more robust plans, work resumed, and the plan to open that August was shelved.

Adjacent to the cathedral site, work was progressing on the bishop's house in Cecil Street. Although the doors were still to be fitted, the bishop and his priests moved in on 23rd September, only to witness another mishap the next day, this time with the newly installed gas lighting and heating: "the plumber applied a candle, when a flame and explosion as from a cannon's mouth burst forth from under him. The glass in the large hall window fell out and the hall was filled with a cloud of falling mortar. Men were everywhere about and the bishop was looking on close by at the operation, but no one was hurt on this Feast of Our Lady. A large piece of loosened wood from the stairs was hurled up near the bishop's head, and has left a deep dent still to be seen on the staircase just above where he was standing." Another close shave, but apparently the last serious problem, and it is notable that, given the size of the project, not one person was killed or even seriously injured during the building.

The organ of Plymouth Cathedral, built in 1799 for the Church of St Martin In the Fields in London.

With the shell of the building complete, work on the interior could begin. The high altar, in Plymouth marble and Caen stone, was installed, Miss Trelawney donated £27 for the stained glass windows in the Blessed Sacrament Chapel, and lights were fitted in the aisle, transepts and clerestories. It is easy to imagine the huge space echoing to the sound of stonemasons at work, and the bishop and his canons dodging the ladders of glaziers and decorators while on their regular rounds of inspection.

One of the last tasks completed was the installation of the organ. The instrument had been built in 1799 by one William Grey for the church of St Martin in the Fields in London at a cost of 600 guineas. It was replaced in 1854, whereupon it was dismantled and put into storage. At a cost of £380 the organ was installed in the Sacred Heart Chapel in the north transept, in time for the organist and choir master M Leopold-de-Prins to practice for the opening.

Building the Cathedral THE FIRST 50 YEARS

The great day was drawing near, and at a meeting attended by the bishop and canons after Chapter Mass in February 1858 it was decided that the opening would be on the Feast of the Annunciation. So, on 25th March, Bishop William Vaughan opened the cathedral with a Pontifical High Mass in the presence of the Cardinal, Provost, the Canons, and priests and worshippers from all over the diocese. In his sermon, the bishop congratulated all those involved in the design and construction, and gave thanks for the absence of any loss of life or limb. The music for the occasion was Weber's *Mass in G*, a piece which would be selected again for the Anniversary Concert in 2008, and proceedings were wound up with the singing of the *Te Deum*.

The speed with which the project had been executed seems astonishing by today's standards, but even in Victorian terms it was a considerable achievement – from conception to opening in less than three years, and with the construction itself taking place in just over two, despite the setback of a major collapse. And yet Bishop Vaughan and his canons could not rest on their laurels, for there was still much to do. A cathedral is never really 'finished' – the building was still very much a work in progress – and there remained a huge task in nurturing the fledgling diocese, for a cathedral is at the heart of the diocese it serves.

Matters administrative, spiritual and practical kept the bishop and his canons busy. On 30th March the church (for thus it still was) was registered for marriages, taking over from the little Chapel of St Mary's which had performed the role for over fifty years, and in February 1861 the church finally became a cathedral.

The most obviously outstanding piece of building left to be completed was the tower and spire. Photographs from the time show a building that, although undeniably impressive, had an unfinished air. The bulk of the nave needed balancing with something finer, more delicate, something that aimed heavenwards and proclaimed the role of the new building. At a cost of £1,500 the tower was erected with the elegant,

The elegant spire of Plymouth Cathedral, 207 feet tall, is a city landmark.

LEFT: Canon Herbert Woollett, first administrator.

PLYMOUTH CATHEDRAL 1858-2008

THE FIRST 50 YEARS

Building the Cathedral

needle-like spire as a worthy finishing touch. At 207ft it was by some distance the highest edifice in Plymouth and immediately became one of the city's landmarks. The bell, known as Peter, was hauled up to its chamber in the tower.

Other, less visible developments took place. In 1859 a pulpit of Caen stone was erected and in 1864 a stone altar, designed by Joseph Hansom, was fixed in the Blessed Sacrament Chapel. In April the same year the Stations of the Cross, made by Philp of London, were erected by Canon Woollett. The caps of the four pillars of the transepts were carved, the Chancel ceiling was decorated, and gas lighting was installed in 1876. Each of these improvements was made possible either by collections (such as the Stations of the Cross, for which Canon Mansfield collected 40 guineas) or the generous donations of individuals. The south wing of the Bishop's House, containing the Dining Room and Library, was completed at a cost of £800 in 1873.

In 1880, Bishop Vaughan celebrated his Episcopal Silver Jubilee with a solemn consecration of the Cathedral on 22nd September, followed by High Mass the next morning.

*1891: The new white stonework of the cathedral's spire dominates this aerial view of Stonehouse and Millbay, drawn from a tethered balloon by Henry William Brewer.
(Plymouth City Museum & Art Gallery).*

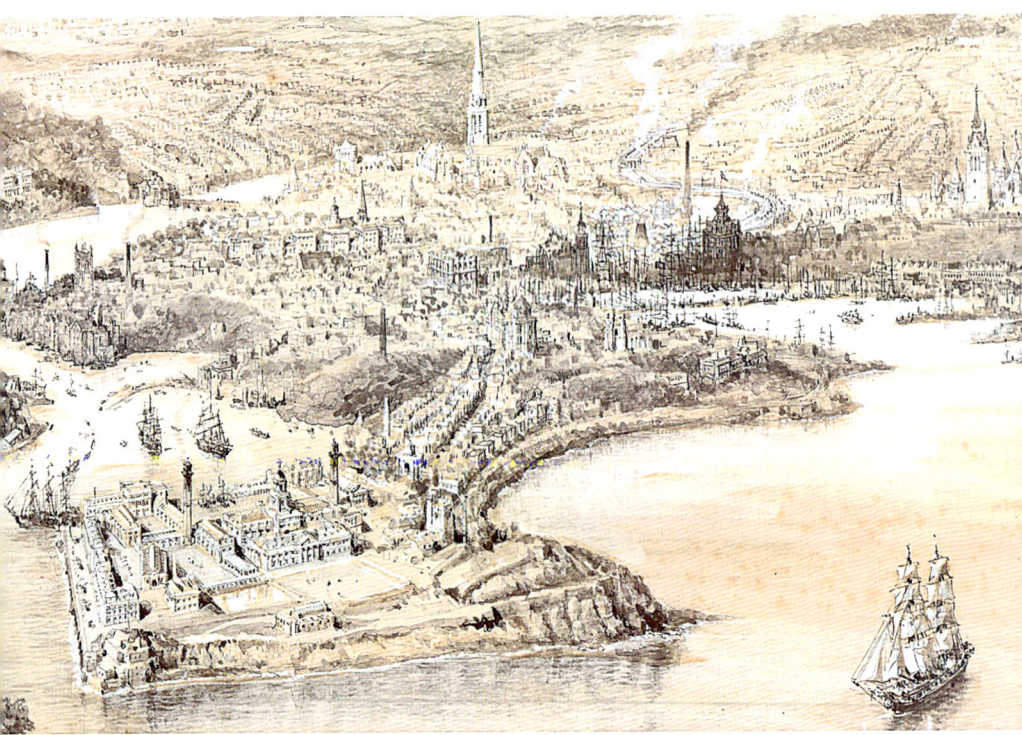

Building the Cathedral
THE FIRST 50 YEARS

The Master of Ceremonies was Canon Charles Graham, who was later to succeed Bishop Vaughan. One of the Jubilee gifts was the stained glass window of St Boniface, installed above the west door. This dramatic window, designed and made by Fouracre and Watson at a cost of £300, shows the figure of St Boniface in the centre light, surrounded by fifteen medallions, each representing a scene from his life.

Eight years later the Bishop celebrated the Golden Jubilee of his priesthood, for which the presentation purse came to £674 and allowed him to embark upon a long-cherished project; the creation of a stone reredos for the high altar. The 30-foot-high reredos, carved of Beer stone and incorporating fourteen marble columns, was sculpted by A B Wall of Cheltenham and installed over three weeks in May 1889.

The original high altar with its 30-foot high reredos of Beer stone installed in 1889.

By now time, and the energies that he had expended on both cathedral and diocese were beginning to take their toll on the health of Bishop Vaughan, and at the age of 78 he suffered a severe illness. He clearly felt he could no longer shoulder the burden alone, and asked Rome for a coadjutor with right of succession. The logical choice was Canon Graham, then the Bishop's Secretary, and he was duly consecrated in the cathedral by the Bishop of Clifton in October 1891.

Although the construction of the cathedral and the continuing improvements had undoubtedly been time-consuming, there were plenty of other, equally important matters to which Bishop Vaughan had attended over the years. By the end of the 19th Century the number of priests had risen to around 100; there were 60 churches, four orphanages, 27 elementary schools and five secondary, 13 houses of male religious and 28 of nuns.

THE FIRST 50 YEARS
Building the Cathedral

The pier at Plymouth's West Hoe around the turn of the century. (Plymouth City Museum & Art Gallery).

1896: New George Street with horse-drawn carriages passing The Royal Theatre on the right and heading towards Derry's Cross.

The changes and advances of the Diocese of Plymouth reflected the changes and advances of the community it served. Plymouth was by now a thriving city, although the three towns of Devonport, Stonehouse and Plymouth (Sutton) were not officially amalgamated until October 1914. It had a smart new pier and promenade on the Hoe, and the beginnings of a tourist industry. There was already John Foulston's Royal Theatre, a fine new library and museum on North Hill, and the elegant new Guildhall, opened on August 13th 1874; all symbols of civic pride and a new affluence.

Building the Cathedral THE FIRST 50 YEARS

A view of the dockyard at the end of the nineteenth century.

Behind the shiny new façade, however, many of the old problems persisted. The dockyard was expanding, its growth spurred by the late Victorian naval arms race; its workforce was in part poorly housed. The Barbican fishing fleet flourished, the trawlers sometimes berthed so closely together it was possible to cross Sutton Pool without getting one's feet wet. The alleys and backstreets of the Barbican were equally crowded, with poor sanitation and few facilities to cater for the gangs of migrant workers who descended on the town with each new season.

> **Despite progress in hygiene and sanitation, disease was still rampant.**

Despite Victorian progress in hygiene and sanitation, disease was still rampant, and while the newly wealthy middle classes flourished and flaunted their finery on the Pier of a balmy evening, the poor were as poor as ever. For many, life was 'nasty, brutish and short'*, and bereft of any spiritual comfort. For all Bishop Vaughan's great accomplishments – and he can truly be seen as the father of both Cathedral and Diocese – as the century drew to its close, there was still much for the Church to do.

* *cf. 'Leviathan' by Thomas Hobbes (17th Cent).*

PLYMOUTH CATHEDRAL 1858-2008

THE FIRST 50 YEARS **Building the Cathedral**

1895: The Chapter of Canons of Plymouth Cathedral. Standing L-R: Remigius Debbault; Thomas Courtenay; William Casey; George Poole; John Tooley; George Hobson; Patrick O'Brien; William Walsh. Seated: L-R Rt Rev Charles Graham Co-adjutor Bishop; His Lordship Bishop William Vaughan; Canon Provost John Laporte. The first Chapter to be photographed.

The Cathedral Chapter

POPE PIUS IX had granted a general permission to the new bishops on 19th November 1850 to select the first members of the chapters of their dioceses. This permission was extended on 6th April 1852 so that the Chapter of Plymouth Cathedral could be 'erected'.

Because there were so few priests in the new diocese (just 23 at its foundation) it was not immediately possible to appoint a full Chapter. So, on 26th November 1853, Bishop Errington selected Dr George Oliver to be the Provost of the new Chapter, with seven canons: Robert Platt of Totnes, Ralph Brindle of Barnstaple, Herbert Woollett of Poole, Maurice Power of Torquay, John Brande Morris of Yealmpton, William Clifford of Stonehouse and Thomas Tilbury of Weymouth.

Since those days there have been many changes. On 10th March 1888, Bishop Vaughan, celebrating the 50th year of his priesthood, increased the number in the Chapter to nine. Similarly Bishop Graham, also on his golden jubilee, completed the Chapter by adding the tenth member; so there was then a Provost and nine canons. This has been the constitution of the Cathedral Chapter ever since.

In 2001, Canon Bartholomew Nannery, the cathedral administrator, was created the first Dean of Plymouth Cathedral.

Canon Christopher Smith

Growth of the Diocese   **THE FIRST 50 YEARS**

Chapter Three

BISHOP VAUGHAN'S enormous labours in building the cathedral were equalled by his work in developing the fledgling Diocese of Plymouth. As we have seen, at the outset of his episcopacy in 1855 there were only 23 priests serving a vast area, and within three years the number had dropped to just 12, and their circumstances were not encouraging.

As late as 1870 Bishop Vaughan was to write, in his Advent pastoral letter: 'Here we find a priest miserably housed, the walls streaming down with wet, there a priest struggling with poverty to support himself and, at the same time, to keep open his Poor-school, even undertaking, for a time, the office of schoolmaster himself rather than allow his children to be scattered. Here again the Holy Sacrifice is offered in an outhouse; many of the

> 'Here we find a priest miserably housed, the walls streaming down with wet, there a priest struggling with poverty to support himself...'

Plymouth Cathedral from the bishop's garden.

THE FIRST 50 YEARS — *Growth of the Diocese*

congregation standing outside in the yard, while those inside are little better accommodated, some being obliged to kneel in the gallery, there being no height to allow them to stand. We visit another mission: there we find all the appliances for the services of religion, but, for months it has been dependent on the charity of a priest living many miles off, who occasionally visits and administers to the flock. Whence has this arisen? The pastor has been struck down by sickness and to the urgent entreaties to appoint a resident pastor, we have had to answer, "We have no priest to send to the Mission"'.

Difficult times, which would have tested the resolve of the strongest faith. But, as one historian noted: ' ...common sense dictated a cautious, make-haste-slowly policy. But Bishop Vaughan, in a moment of high detachment, had detached the common and kept the sense ... he was given a heart full of that Christian courage which is hardly distinguishable from foolhardiness.' This courage would be needed, not only to continue the development of the diocese, but also to address the wider issues of the day.

Cornwall, as always, was suffering; the mining industry was in decline and deprivation was widespread, while nationally, there was social unrest as the embryonic trades union movement flexed its muscles on behalf of the workers, confronting exploitation and poor working conditions. The bishop gave this much thought: '... there is one consequence, resulting from the existing trades' union disputes, that cannot be ignored. They are seriously affecting and injuring the trade of the country; which means nothing less than impoverishing all classes of society. Let each one, in his respective position in life, strive to promote a spirit of kindliness and mutual forebearance under provocation, knowing that where passion or party spirit gains the ascendancy, justice and charity are cast aside, and injury, if not ruin, is the penalty to be paid... "for a house divided against itself cannot stand." ' Bishop Vaughan was not the only churchman to be concerned, and the great social reformer Cardinal Manning became involved in 1889 when he was instrumental in settling the London dock strike.

Then there was the 'Irish Question'. The forced migration caused by the potato famine had greatly swelled the number of

1887: Strikers and police clash in Trafalgar Square, London on Bloody Sunday.
(TUC Library Collections)

Growth of the Diocese

THE FIRST 50 YEARS

Irish in Britain; firmly rooted at the bottom of the social hierarchy, occupying jobs in construction and shipping, they provided a ready source of cheap labour and, in times of economic downturn, were first in line for redundancy. They had their champions, chief among whom was Cardinal Manning, but there was an unfortunate attitude towards the Irish even from fellow Catholics, as demonstrated by a comment from a Mrs Charlton in 1860.

Trying to ease the embarrassment caused by anti-Catholic remarks at his dinner table, the Marquis of Westminster pointed out that Mrs Charlton was a Catholic, to which she replied: 'Yes, but an English Catholic, not an Irish one, which is all the difference in the world. English Catholics are responsible beings who are taught right from wrong, whereas Irish Catholics, belonging to a yet savage nation, know no better and are perhaps excusable on that account.' Attitudes like this did nothing to help the lot of the Irish Catholics and they, on their part, nurtured an understandable hostility to the English and particularly the absentee landlords whose neglect and exploitation of their tenants was a direct cause of the migration. Another event indicative of the fact that society's attitude towards Catholicism was not all it might have been was the reception into the faith of the famous poet and vicar of Morwenstow Robert Hawker on his death bed at Plymouth in 1875. 'Feeling ran high in this town for the soreness amongst Protestants were most painful', wrote Bishop Kiely some years later.

1875: Reverend Robert Stephen Hawker, the celebrated Vicar of Morwenstow, became a Catholic on his death bed.

The Church occupied a position bestriding English and Irish, rich and poor, the exploiters and the downtrodden. Bishop Vaughan was faced with an uphill task in providing spiritual and temporal sustenance for all of his flock, whatever their station. His pastoral letters provide an insight into both the problems that occupied his mind and their gradual solution. And 'gradual' the process had to be for, as one historian noted: 'The missions lived from hand to mouth, and it had to be a dexterous hand and not too large a mouth.'

It was, of course, too large a task even for the broad shoulders of Bishop Vaughan, but he was supported in his labours by an able group of men of God: Canon Henry Woollett, for example, the first canon administrator of the Cathedral and Vicar-General of the diocese, who served under Bishop Vaughan for

PLYMOUTH CATHEDRAL 1858-2008

THE FIRST 50 YEARS — *Growth of the Diocese*

over forty years, and Canon Charles Graham, the bishop's secretary. There was Monsignor Brindle, provost of the cathedral Chapter, who laboured tirelessly for the Catholics of Barnstaple, and his namesake Rev Father Ambrose Brindle, who was confessor to St Augustine's Priory at Newton Abbot. Rev Thomas Spencer at Ilfracombe, Rev Patrick O'Brien at Devonport, and Rev William Downing at Dartmouth all played their part under the guidance of Bishop Vaughan, as did many others too numerous to mention. The laity likewise made their contributions, people like the dowager Lady Clifford, Sir Frederick Weld of Chideock, John Lewis Harding, and Richard Lerins de Bary of Sclerder.

Far and wide across Cornwall, Devon and Dorset, piece by piece, the infrastructure of the diocese grew. In the 1860s, sites were secured and chapels commenced at Portland, Dartmouth and Dorchester. Falmouth, Truro, West Lulworth, all saw the building of churches or chapels, in the latter case with a school attached. A new church of St Michael and St Joseph in Devonport was opened by the Bishop in 1861, and twenty years later Plymouth received its third mission – Holy Cross – in somewhat unusual circumstances. 'The Church of Our Lady and St Charles Borromeo at Teignmouth having to be taken down for railway improvements, the materials were bought up by the Bishop of Plymouth and brought to Tothill Lane Plymouth for the building of this Church of 'The Holy Cross'. The same foundation stone, laid at Teignmouth on 13 July 1854 was blessed and placed here on 15 April 1881. The contractors for the building were Messrs Hayman of Teignmouth, sons of the late Mr Hayman who built the original church at Teignmouth.'

The Convent School of Notre Dame, founded in 1864 and built next to the cathedral.

The orphanage at St Marychurch, providing accommodation for sixty orphans, was completed in 1867. The needs of the young were an important consideration, laying foundations for the future of the Faith, and this is reflected in the development of Catholic education in the diocese. As early as 1852 Bishop Errington had opened a school at Granby Street, which later moved to Chapel Street. In 1860, at the invitation of the Bishop, six Sisters of Notre Dame

Growth of the Diocese

THE FIRST 50 YEARS

arrived in Plymouth and took over a house formerly occupied by priests in Stonehouse as their convent, where they also opened a day school. In 1863 the Reverend Mother General deemed the Stonehouse premises too drab and unhealthy and as a result, in November 1864 the foundation stone of the new convent was laid in Wyndham Street adjacent to the Cathedral. By 1880 the Convent of Notre Dame was providing schooling for over 600 children.

In other areas, due to local privations, development was, of necessity, less ambitious. The Bishop writes in 1870: 'We staved off poverty from the door and supplied the means to pay for the moment the Schoolmistress at Camborne.'

As well as the needs of the flock, those of the priests were not ignored. Early in his episcopacy, Bishop Vaughan set up the Secular Clergy Fund to cater for the needs of sick and aged priests for, as he said, 'who are more deserving in the decline of age and privation of health, than those priests, who have spent their best days ministering to others?' More immediate priestly needs were met by the building of presbyteries, although this was not always as immediately accomplished as might have been hoped: in the 1870s, the Bishop writes that 'We sent workmen into the priest's house at Liskeard to make it habitable', and it was not until 1880 that, 'through the generosity of a kind benefactor, the enlargement and improvement of the presbytery at Liskeard has been effected.'

Bishop Vaughan set up the Secular Clergy Fund, saying: '...who are more deserving ... than those priests who have spent their best days ministering to others?'

St Mary's Abbey, Buckfast showing part of the ancient foundations.

1884 was to see in the diocese an event of national importance. The Benedictine Monks of Pierre-qui-vire, in France, were expelled by the French government, and purchased a property near Buckfastleigh which contained within its boundary the site of the old Cistercian Monastery of Buckfast. The Abbot's Tower was restored and excavations laid bare the foundations of the ancient Abbey, which were used to support the new building. It was, as Bishop Vaughan wrote in his Pastoral Letter of 1885, 'the first attempt to reconstruct on its original lines a pre-reformation Abbey.'

THE FIRST 50 YEARS *Growth of the Diocese*

Bishop William Vaughan in later years.

While great works were going on there were other, more mundane matters to attend to. In 1882 a fire gutted the Presbyterian Chapel in Wyndham Street and severely damaged part of the adjoining Convent of Notre Dame, and in 1885 the Cathedral was struck by lightning, damaging all the gutters and downpipes. In this case, the West of England Fire Insurance Company footed the bill, but not all outgoings were so readily met: 'In consequence of the weather-cock becoming fixed, the upper stones of the steeple were injured, and had to be made good: and, the pointing being defective, We decided, as the ladders were in position, to re-point the Spire. This will, we feel sure, secure the stability of this elegant structure for very many years.' The cost was eighty pounds – less than a day's labour at today's prices.

Archbishop Errington, founder of the diocese and Bishop Vaughan's predecessor, died in 1886, leaving £100 to the diocese for the purpose of educating students. Two years later the first Canon of the Cathedral, and Vicar-General, Very Rev Canon Herbert Woollett died and was replaced by Very Rev Canon Brownlow from St Marychurch. In 1893 Bishop William Clifford, former Vicar General to Bishop Errington, died after thirty six years as Bishop of Clifton.

The redoubtable Bishop Vaughan was still busy at the age of 77, travelling hither and yon throughout the diocese, but time – and the British weather – eventually caught up with him. The winter of 1891 is famous for its ferocity; snow started falling in November and remained in places on the ground until May. There was a brief respite in February, and the Bishop took the chance to make a visitation of St Augustine's Priory at Newton Abbot, where he caught a cold. The following day, although feeling unwell, he confirmed 130 candidates at the cathedral and it is recorded that the number of communicants through the three towns was 2,200 – a huge increase from the 13 Catholics recorded in the Bishop of Exeter's 1767 census. On 22nd February 1892 Bishop Vaughan came down with a fever and was confined to his bed for five weeks. He recovered sufficiently to say Mass on Easter Sunday, but the illness had left a lasting weakness, and 'a thought, that had for some time been floating in Our mind, forced itself then as a fixed resolve.' He applied for a Coadjutor, with right of succession. Rome grant-

Growth of the Diocese **THE FIRST 50 YEARS**

ed its leave the same year on 13th June, and on 1st July the Chapter, at a special meeting after Mass, selected three names to forward to the Holy See. On 3rd September 1892 news was received that Canon Graham had been elected coadjutor, and three weeks later he was constituted titular Bishop of Cisamus with right of succession to the Bishopric of Plymouth. Bishop Clifford of Clifton, assisted by Bishop Knight of Shrewsbury and Bishop Vertue of Portsmouth, performed the consecration at the Cathedral on 28th October. The service was attended by most of the clergy of the diocese and representatives of all the religious orders, and lunch for 72 was enjoyed afterwards in the dining hall of the Bishop's House.

Bishop Vaughan was pleased to have one of his protegés step into his shoes: 'To Us personally this appointment has been most acceptable . . . We have known him from his childhood, and have found him most indefatigable in his labours for the diocese during his Priesthood of over thirty years; and We know full well that his heartfelt desires are, and have been, to devote all his energies to the best interests of the diocese.' So it was that Bishop Vaughan retired to St Augustine's Priory in Newton Abbot early in 1892 but returned to Plymouth regularly.

Bishop Charles Graham, third Bishop of Plymouth.

Bishop Graham was immediately busy, confirming 81 candidates in October. The following year Mgr Brownlow, the Vicar-General, was appointed to the vacant Provostship of the cathedral Chapter. In 1894 he became Bishop of Clifton, and in this capacity was invited back to the Cathedral to bless and erect the new Stations of the Cross for which he had been largely responsible for raising the funds. In the same year the churches of The Sacred Heart in Bideford and The Star of the Sea in Ilfracombe were opened, the foundations of St Aldhelm at Sherborne were laid and, also at Sherborne, the Sisters of Christian Instruction opened 'A higher and middle class girls' school, also a day school for the poor.'

The business of the diocese, major and minor, continued unabated under the old bishop and his new coadjutor. Bishop Graham said Mass in July 1895 aboard the flagship of Admiral

THE FIRST 50 YEARS   *Growth of the Diocese*

Spinosa of the Spanish fleet while at anchor in Plymouth Sound (what would Drake have made of that, one wonders?), and Bishop Vaughan hosted the 5th Diocesan Synod at the Cathedral shortly after. In 1898 the spire of the Cathedral was again hit by lightning, destroying the new electric clock. A Collegiate School was set up at 31 Wyndham Street under Rev Michael Burns of the English College in Valladolid in 1900.

Early in June of 1902, Bishop Vaughan made his final visit to the cathedral.

Early in June of 1902 Bishop Vaughan made his fourth and final visit to the Cathedral. He gave parting gifts to clergy and friends, and made a short, valedictory address at evening service on 8th June. He died peacefully on 25th October at St Augustine's, and his body was buried there on 31st October after a Pontifical High Mass at the Cathedral.

Bishop Graham's work has, perhaps inevitably, been characterised as being so intertwined with that of his predecessor as to be almost indistinguishable, but this a little unfair. As coadjutor to the ailing Bishop Vaughan he carried his share of the episcopal burden, and on succeeding to Plymouth he did not rest on his laurels.

During his bishopric there were eight new churches opened, including St Edward's at Peverell, along with three Mass centres, and the college in Wyndham Square was expanded. He was also and avid recorder of events in the diocese, leaving behind an invaluable resource for historians. Bishop Graham's tenure lasted a mere eight years; in 1910 he fell seriously ill and retired to Hayle where, in the care of the Daughters of the Cross, he died on 2nd September 1911.

BELOW: Bishop Vaughan's memorial brass tablet in the south transept.

Growth of the Diocese **THE FIRST 50 YEARS**

Canon Patrick Sheehan (1852-1913)

ONE OF THE Cathedral's early curates, a man set to acquire distinction in the literary field later, was Patrick Sheehan. Ordained in 1875 for the Diocese of Cloyne, Co Cork, he had no parish to go to at home and was lent to Bishop Vaughan. He began his priestly duties at the Cathedral in the summer of 1875, living at Bishop's House. His experiences there as curate to the formidable William Vaughan game him material for his novel "Luke Delmege". In 1876 he was moved to Exeter and there gained a reputation as a powerful preacher, some of his sermons being recalled by elderly parishioners almost fifty years later so lasting was his impression on them.

A spell as temporary chaplain to Dartmoor Prison is reflected in his descriptions of the fettered convicts being led to their labours at the Merrivale granite quarry. They form some of the most vivid depictions of the lot of the Victorian convict in his book on the Fenian Rising of 1867 in "The Graves at Kilmorna".

He was recalled by his bishop in 1877 after only two years but his experiences and what he had learned from them were to have a lasting impact on the rest of his life and ministry. As curate in the naval base of Queenstown (now Cobh) in the 1880s, his training in Plymouth stood him in good stead in ministering to sailors many of whom were Irish Catholics. Bishop's Vaughan's lifelong crusade to raise the social status of his flock was adapted by Sheehan in his campaign to raise the economic prospects of his parishioners. He was ever active in schemes to improve the economic fabric of the country and, in later years when his success as a novelist brought him, a substantial income, he was quick to use this wealth to improve the lives of his flock. Novels like "Glenanaar", "The Blindness of Dr Gray" and "The Graves at Kilmorna" had substantial sales in these islands and in the USA.

Canon Sheehan's curacy in Plymouth made him realise that the need to reconcile people of different faiths was of paramount importance. He was particularly anxious to ensure that the movement towards Irish Home Rule should not take on a sectarian character and he was very active in campaigns to take sectarianism out of politics. He did not live to see what he feared so acutely, the partition of Ireland in 1921 which, ultimately, gave rise to the Northern Ireland Troubles of the past forty years.

Canon Sheehan may have spent just two years among us but these were formative years for the young curate and their impact would be lifelong.   ***Tom Healy***

THE FIRST 50 YEARS *Growth of the Diocese*

This magnificent stained glass window in the south transept is a memorial to Bishop William Vaughan.

The First World War

THE TWO WORLD WARS

PART II ~ *The Two World Wars.*

Chapter Four

BISHOP GRAHAM'S successor, and the fourth Bishop of Plymouth, was John Joseph Keily. Born in Limerick in 1854, he was ordained at Plymouth Cathedral in 1877 and went on to hold the post of Diocesan Inspector of Schools. He was highly regarded as a preacher, filling churches all over the diocese, and was memorably described by one commentator as being 'one of the few bishops who did not look as if the mitre were several sizes too big.' Monsignor Barry mentioned his 'princely bearing'. He became a Canon in 1897 and was consecrated Bishop of Plymouth by Cardinal Bourne in 1911.

One of the first big events organised by Bishop Keily was the annual meeting of the Catholic Young Men's Society (CYMS) in the Royal Theatre in 1912. Originally based at the Hibernia Institute on Belmont Street, the CYMS soon moved to the new parochial buildings on Cecil Street, which boasted a fine concert hall, a billiards room, a (soft drinks only!) bar, a library and a card room.

Bishop John Keily.

The bishop with the cathedral Chapter.

THE TWO WORLD WARS — The First World War

> '...you mention it and the Cathedral parish had it.'

The CYMS was but one of many organisations active in the life of the Diocese – there were also the Catenians, the Boys' Brigade, the Children of Mary, the St Vincent de Paul Society, the Society of the Blessed Sacrament ... in the words of Herbert C. Woodman, 'you mention it and the Cathedral parish had it. It ran its own celebrity concerts in the Parochial Hall, steamer trips to places like Weir Head, Calstock and Cawsand, train trips to beauty spots on the moor like Shaugh Bridge, Clearbrook and Yelverton. The CYMS had its own adventure section that taught young men to row and sail their two 32ft naval sailing ships on evening trips with members of the Children of Mary.'

With a new cathedral hall at his disposal, Bishop Keily's next coup was to secure the Fourth National Catholic Congress for Plymouth in 1913. A veritable bevy of Bishops greeted the President of the Congress, Cardinal Bourne, as he alighted from his train at 2.35 p.m. on 4th July, and an address of welcome was made by Lord Clifford of Chudleigh. That evening there was a Great Mass Meeting at the Guildhall, attended by all the Bishops, a host of clergy and laity, and his worship the Mayor of Plymouth, J. W. E. Godding. Tickets cost 10/6 for a reserved seat (through Door A), 2/6 at Door B and 1/- at Door C; the door through which you entered was presumably decided on the basis of social class! Hymns were sung, and the Band of the Royal Garrison Artillery played a selection of music by Massenet, Mendelssohn and others, and proceedings were rounded off with God Save the King. For the next three days there was a dizzying round of services, meetings and functions, attended by Catholics from all over the country. The Catholic Boys' Brigade, resplendent in their dress uniforms, acted as messengers, and medals with red ribbons were presented to all Catholic schoolchildren. The final event was a meeting at the Guildhall, organised by the Catholic Truth Society on the subject of 'Religion in Modern England', at which the speakers were Rev C. C. Martindale S. J. and Right Rev Mgr Bickerstaffe-Drew. Proceedings were rounded off with

1913: The Handbook of the Fourth National Catholic Congress. (Frank Payne)

The First World War **THE TWO WORLD WARS**

the Mayor 'At Home' to the Congress in the Guildhall, and the following day, as light relief, there were 'Excursions to various places of interest.' The Plymouth Diocese had truly arrived on the national stage.

With the departure of the delegates, life could return to normal, and the diocese continued about its business, buoyed up by the memory of august personages, lively debates and memorable ceremonies. Through all this vibrant activity strode the imposing yet approachable figure of Bishop Keily, often to be seen holding the hand of a small child or chatting with members of his flock. He looked after his priests, too – 'many an impecunious curate going on holiday forgot the near decapitation of his toes when the tall Bishop, wishing him the best of a good time, shook hands with him ... in shaking hands His Lordship slips a £5 note into the departing curate's hand; the curate is expected to act as if nothing had happened. There were many red-letter days with the open-handed Bishop.' None of God's creatures seemed to escape his notice. Once, on a visit to London 'He was leaving one of our largest churches after saying Mass, when a cat in difficulties attracted his attention. In trying to escape the unwelcome overtures of a small but pugnacious dog, the cat attempted to get into the church, and thereby risked being injured by the revolving doors. The Bishop immediately stooped, picked up puss, and drove off the intruder. Not until the danger was past did the kindly Bishop set down the frightened animal, who showed her gratitude by following him some distance, until she herself had to be "shooshed" back in friendly fashion.'

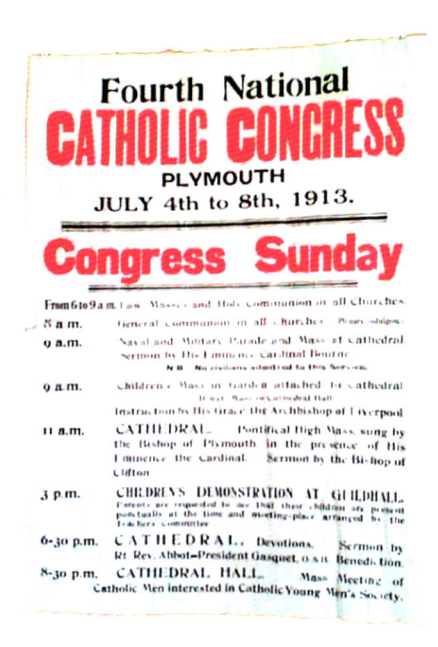

1913: One of the posters for the Congress with a timetable of events.

His affability and generosity masked a sterner side, however: one commentator remarked that 'He could put his foot down with crushing effect when necessary'. Another recalled 'a rigidity behind his affable exterior which, since it related to his religious faith, called for respect, or even admiration, but did not help to round off the corners or soften the asperities of intercourse with fellow-townsmen whose faith and belief differed from his.' In the light of this it is remarkable that one of his closest friends was Rev Benwell Bird of the Free Church.

THE TWO WORLD WARS   The First World War

Bishop Keily's flock in the first two decades of the 20th century was composed in the main of three different groups. There were English Catholics who could trace their ancestry back through the generations to Irish roots – families such as the Woodmans, the Armstrongs, the Turnstalls, the Featherstones and the Kingwells. The next group were also of Irish origin, but had arrived more recently as a result of the potato famine - the Kellys, the Rileys, and the Durneys. Lastly there were Italian families such as the Trefannis, the Policellas, the Buchinnis and the Pretes.

For the families of Irish origin the years 1912 - 25 were difficult ones, testing their faith and loyalties. The vexed 'Irish Question' had never gone away and during these years was to come to a bloody, confusing climax. The Third Home Rule Bill, approved by Parliament in April 1912 for enactment in 1914, led directly to the formation of the Protestant Ulster Volunteer Force, opposed to any imposition of Home Rule. Sinn Fein – formed in 1905 – were also opposed to Home Rule, but their opposition stemmed from a desire to see a fully independent Ireland. However, as 1914 dawned, international attention turned towards the inevitability of war in Europe; the Irish Question would have to wait.

The Royal Naval Hospital, near the cathedral, cared for many wartime casualties. (Steve Johnson)

The tens of thousands of headstones that mark the deaths of men at battles like Somme and Ypres are symbolic of the great folly of World War One, and indeed many soldiers from Plymouth rest in Flanders fields, but less considered are the naval casualties. As one of the major naval ports of the empire, Plymouth contributed thousands of men and hundreds of ships to the war effort. The first Plymouth ship to founder was HMS Amphion, which struck a mine off Harwich on August 5th 1914, and thereafter every month brought news of the loss of a local ship and the decimation of its crew. Plymouth ships fought in every theatre of the war: four battleships were lost in two months in 1915 at the Dardanelles; HMS Defence, HMS Nomad, HMS Indefatigable and HMS Warrior all fell to the German High Seas Fleet at Jutland in 1916, where Admiral Beattie's

The First World War

THE TWO WORLD WARS

flagship HMS Lion stayed afloat by the skin of her teeth; HMS Pegasus was sunk off Zanzibar. In all, from the 18,750 ton Indefatigable to the armed yacht Rhianon of a mere 138 tons, 95 Plymouth ships were lost. Hundreds more were damaged and the casualties among Plymouth men ran into thousands. The Royal Naval Hospital (RNH) in Stonehouse was bursting at the seams, and every naval household dreaded the arrival at the door of the 'telegram boy' bearing bad news from the Admiralty, especially in the aftermath of major actions such as Jutland or the Dardanelles.

In these dreadful circumstances – with every other house suffering the loss, maiming or disablement by 'shell shock' of a son, father, brother, cousin or uncle – Catholic priests and sisters provided much needed support. The constant round of visits to grief-stricken families must have been wearing for the priests, who found their faith being questioned and tested, while for the nuns and sisters, who gave unstintingly of their time to assist in tending the wounded at RNH Stonehouse, the sights and smells of so much dismemberment and despair had to be borne with a smile and unshakeable faith.

In the absence of any sort of welfare state families had to fall back on the generosity of friends and fellow parishioners, and the strong sense of community of the Cathedral parish was tested but never failed.

Into these trying times, in 1916, was added a further pressure from a quarter that had, it appeared (to those who felt out of sight was out of mind) slipped quietly offstage. Encouraged by the fact that the war was going badly for the Allies, and hoping the authorities had taken their eye off the ball, nearly 1,000 rebels from the Irish Volunteers proclaimed an Irish Republic

> **Every naval household dreaded the arrival at the door of the 'telegram boy' ... especially after major battles.**

1916: Members of the Irish Volunteers join the Easter rising in Dublin. (okelly.net)

PLYMOUTH CATHEDRAL 1858-2008

35

THE TWO WORLD WARS The First World War

and, under the leadership of Pádraic Pearse and James Connolly, seized Dublin's General Post Office on Easter Monday. Troops poured into Dublin and gunboats shelled the rebels from the River Liffey. In five days the fighting was over at a cost of 400 deaths and 2,500 injured, and the rebels surrendered. Retribution was swift, with fifteen of the rebels executed in May, and in Britain the spectre of anti-Irish hatred raised its head again. As is the way with these things, the sentiments raised were less than balanced, commonly ignoring the fact that thousands of Irish troops had died and were still dying fighting for the King in all the theatres of war.

The Catholic community was on the receiving end of a lot of criticism and downright hostility and Bishop Keily found himself walking a difficult tightrope, caught between his natural sympathy for his troubled homeland and his wider duty to church and flock. He must have been a natural diplomat, for he '… came out of those testing years with banners flying. He left no dead friendships, English or Irish, on the field. No act or word of his turned his fold into a hostile camp. He left no doubts in anyone's mind that he was an Irishman and a great Irishman.'

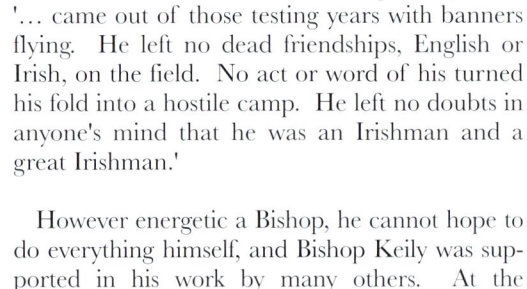

However energetic a Bishop, he cannot hope to do everything himself, and Bishop Keily was supported in his work by many others. At the Cathedral there were – to name but a few – Canon Cyril Mahoney (Administrator from 1923), Revs Burke and Morrissey, who acted as Secretary and Treasurer to the Catholic Congress, and Canon Ford and Rev McGuigan, both in their time Choir Chaplains. At outlying parishes were men like Rev Edward Dewey of Devonport, Rev David Barry (Holy Cross), and Rev (later Canon) Walter Gaynor at Keyham. On the lay side were the headmistress of the girls' school, Sister Mary (or 'tall Sister Mary', as the children called her to distinguish her from her smaller namesake at the infants' school), with her staff the Misses Dustin, Gurowitch, Gick and O'Flaherty; Mr McCarthy, head at the boys' school and also assistant organist, and his staff who included Mr J Dustin, killed in action during the war. This is merely a selection of names, of course. There were hundreds of others – priests and parishioners, sisters and secretaries, cleaners, gardeners and organ blowers – who all played their part in ensuring that the Cathedral and the Diocese came through a difficult time stronger and more confident.

Rt Rev Monsignor Canon Cyril Mahoney, Vicar General and administrator of the cathedral.

The First World War   **THE TWO WORLD WARS**

IN REFRIGERIUM ÆTERNUM
ET PIAM MEMORIAM FRATRUM
CARISSIMORUM QUI TERRA
MARIQUE MORTUI SUNT
MCMXIV – MCMXVIII.
HOC SACELLUM CUM ALTARI
IN HONOREM IMMACULATÆ
VIRGINIS MARIÆ FIDELES
MOERENTES PONENTES DICARUNT
O CLEMENS: O PIA: O DULCIS
VIRGO MARIA

The war memorial now in the Peace Chapel of St Patrick and St George.

PLYMOUTH CATHEDRAL 1858-2008   37

THE TWO WORLD WARS — The First World War

Lord Clifford of Chudleigh, Chairman of the Committee for the Fourth National Catholic Congress, held in Plymouth in 1913. He is dressed in the uniform of a Count of The Holy Roman Empire.

The 1920s and 30s   **THE TWO WORLD WARS**

Chapter Five

WHEN THE GUNS finally fell silent in November 1918, over a million British servicemen had died, and countless others were disabled. Although Europe was at peace for the first time in four years, the war had eroded some of the old social order and change was in the air. For the first time, appreciable numbers of women were entering the workforce in a professional capacity – education, for example, where a shortage of available men meant that in primary schools, at least, women teachers outnumbered their male counterparts.

The troubles in Ireland rumbled on, with the Black and Tans, raised by the Government from ex-servicemen, exacting retribution for the actions of the fledgling IRA and fuelling resentment among Irish Catholics. The fall of the Romanovs in Russia, and the subsequent rise to power of Lenin's Communist party was giving governments all over the continent the jitters and the spectre of revolution haunted the thoughts of the old guard. In Britain the Labour Party, with a post-war membership of over four million, was a power to be reckoned with, further shaking the confidence of an establishment that not, by and large, distinguished itself during the war.

1919: Cardinal Francis Bourne (with mitre) pictured at the consecration of the new Carmelite monastery at Efford Manor, Plymouth.

Times were uneasy, but the normality of the everyday must have been reassuring. On July 30th 1920, the *Universe* reported four events from the Diocese of Plymouth. At Hayle, a garden fête was held in the grounds of St Michael's Hospital, opened by Lady Carkeek and featuring 'Excellent arrangements by Mrs E Ellis and Mrs Hedley Simmons.' The event raised £150 for the Daughters of the Cross.

THE TWO WORLD WARS — *The 1920s and 30s*

1925: The newly completed Blessed Sacrament Chapel is consecrated by Bishop John Keily.

The Forty Hours' Devotion was begun at St Edward the Martyr in Shaftesbury, while in Plymouth Bishop Kiely hosted a garden party. The list of stallholders provides an insight into the composition of the flock: 'Mesdames Pengelly, Pearce, Hallihan, Keys, Leahy, Browning, Hudd, Bucchini, Johnstone, Boadi, Herbert, Kiely, Norris, Boyes-Fowler, and the Misses O'Reilly, Binney and Foster-Bone.' On a less happy note, it was reported that the parish of Marnhull was passing through a critical stage, brought on by the gradual departure of the congregation and Father Dodard was said to be in a 'desperate position'.

In 1920 Partition was introduced to Ireland, a solution that pleased neither Republicans nor Unionists but did pave the way for the Irish Free State Treaty of 1921 and the Civil War the following year. Pius XI became Pope in 1922, and the first Labour Government, led by Ramsay Macdonald, was elected in 1924. 1926 saw the upheaval of the National Strike and, in its wake, a message of reconciliation from Bishop Keily: 'We have

2008: Exposition of the Blessed Sacrament, 9.30am - 4.45pm Monday - Thursday and up to 7pm Friday; also Saturday 10.30am - 4pm in this lovely chapel.

PLYMOUTH CONSECRATION.

1858-2008 PLYMOUTH CATHEDRAL

The 1920s and 30s

to gather up the broken fragments of industry and get to work again . . . Nothing can be more unthinkable just now than swagger of success or coarse recrimination. A neighbour's loss is no gain; and therefore our right state of mind is just hearty thanks to God who has brought us out of great peril and not a little sorrow for families who must certainly bear the dead weight of the trouble.'

Great events, and in particular the travails of his homeland, must have been a heavy burden to Bishop Keily, but he bore them with his usual fortitude and tact, and continued the more mundane but no less important matters of the Diocese.

The Lady Chapel was remodelled to become the Diocesan War Memorial, the High Altar was changed, and the choir gallery across the north transept was moved. The organ (still the original one from St Martin in the Fields) was rebuilt by Hele's of Milehouse and moved to the former Sacred Heart Chapel. This work was overseen by Bernard O'Brien, a builder, and Master of Ceremonies on the altar, who was later made a Papal Count for his services to the Church.

Bishop Keily was not ignored when it came to honours, either: in 1927 Pope Pius XI conferred upon him the dignity of Bishop Assistant at the Pontifical Throne in recognition of a life spent in the service of the Church and the Diocese. In March of that

THE TWO WORLD WARS

Bishop Keily celebrated his golden jubilee in 1927 and was presented with this £2000 cheque.

THE TWO WORLD WARS — The 1920s and 30s

The funeral procession of Bishop Keily passes through the streets of Plymouth while the priests recite the Rosary.

year he celebrated the golden jubilee of his ordination with a Mass at the Cathedral, and was presented with a cheque for £2,000 by Mr Edward Tozer. The following year, on 23rd September, Bishop Keily died at the age of 74. He had been Bishop for 17 years, through a period of great turbulence and change – war, the Irish Troubles, the 1926 Catholic Emancipation Act and the General Strike – and the tributes to him were fulsome and many, both from the laity and from clergy of all denominations. One of the simplest yet most eloquent was from Herbert C Woodman, who wrote: 'I, with many others, saw him lying in state in the severe small bedroom of his palace. He was a most humble man and the experience of knowing him has lasted through the whole of my lifetime, for my spiritual good and comfort.'

> **The tributes to Bishop Keily were fulsome and many, both from the laity and from clergy of all denominations.**

John Patrick Barrett, Bishop Kiely's successor, was born in Liverpool in 1878. He was ordained in 1906, studied at the Beda College in Rome, where he took degrees in Divinity and Philosophy, and later became a Professor of Moral Theology. On 22nd February 1927 he was consecrated bishop at Birmingham, and on 7th June 1929 he transferred to Plymouth.

Despite his scholarliness, Bishop Barrett is remembered as an

The 1920s and 30s — THE TWO WORLD WARS

approachable, affable man: 'Priests and children were equally at ease with him, with or without the passport of an appointment... His completely unaffected homeliness was, perhaps, the most endearing of his many endearing qualities.' He was short-sighted, possibly as a result of many years in dimly lit libraries: 'He might not see too clearly the white lines or the cat's eyes on a road – sitting beside him had more than the hair-raising thrills of a taxi ride in Paris – but he never took a wrong turning on any road, and could see further round life's corners than most men . . . He had a keen palate for red wine and Lancashire hot-pot. He loved priests with problems and children with games.' (sic)

Like his predecessor, Bishop Barrett's time in office was marked by turbulence in the tide of world events. The Wall Street Crash took place only months after his arrival in Plymouth, and the ensuing world wide depression would savage economies, put men out of work and fuel the rise of Fascism.

1929: The enthronement of Bishop John Barrett was front page news.

THE TWO WORLD WARS

The 1920s and 30s

Events in the life of a Cathedral come in all shapes and sizes. Almost the first thing that Bishop Barrett had to deal with was the fate of the great bell known as Peter, which had become cracked. It was removed, but a replacement would not be found for many years.

The first big occasion of Bishop Barrett's episcopate was the golden jubilee of the consecration of the Cathedral, celebrated on September 22nd 1930 with a Pontifical High Mass presided over by the Metropolitan of the Birmingham Province, Archbishop Thomas Williams – the man who, three years earlier, had consecrated Bishop Barrett. The sermon was preached by Father Anscar Vonier, Abbot of Buckfast.

St Paul's church in St Budeaux was blessed by Bishop Barrett in 1933.

Plymouth was at this time expanding into the countryside and the population grew with it; Catholics formed part of this growth and there was a demand for more churches and schools.

The first of the thirties churches was Our Lady of Lourdes at Plympton, built on Vicarage Road in memory of Bishop Keily. When it opened on May 18th 1932, Our Lady of Lourdes marked the re-establishment of a Catholic presence for the first time since the Reformation, when the old Priory of St Mary, once a major power in the area, was dissolved. St Budeaux's historical legacy went back even further to St Budoc, one of the first Christian missionaries to the South West, and now it was to receive its own Catholic church through the generosity of two Lancashire spinsters, the Robinsons. St Paul's on Pemros Road was blessed by Bishop Barrett on 5th November 1933. At Plymstock, the Church of St Gregory the Great was opened in 1933, a chapel of ease served by the Holy Cross Parish, and another chapel of ease opened in 1937 at Crownhill to serve the growing army garrison.

The first big occasion of Bishop Barrett's episcopate was the golden jubilee of the consecration of the cathedral.

1858-2008 PLYMOUTH CATHEDRAL

The 1920s and 30s   **THE TWO WORLD WARS**

Beaconfield in the 1970s.

Bishop John Barrett, fifth Bishop of Plymouth.

In January 1931, at the instigation of Bishop Barrett, a new secondary school was opened on the Cathedral school site for older children from the Cathedral, Devonport and Holy Cross parishes, and a separate secondary school was established to serve the Keyham parish. A group of Presentation Sisters set up a preparatory school at Beechfield, Hartley, in 1933, while in St Budeaux, St Paul's School was opened in September 1935, staffed by the Notre Dame Sisters.

The Irish Presentation Brothers, who had run St Boniface's College since 1916, were leaving, but Bishop Barrett invited the Irish Christian Brothers to take over and on 7th September 1931 the college re-opened in new premises at Beaconfield under the headship of Brother McDonald, with 142 pupils. He said that the new college was a great change for the better from the old school in Wyndham Square where the Presentation Brothers had worked so earnestly and successfully.

1931: Bishop Barrett opened the new Saint Boniface's College at Beaconfield.

Education and church building were not the only areas of growth, however. Religious orders were expanding and in 1931 the Poor Sisters of Nazareth arrived from Exeter to set up an

THE TWO WORLD WARS   *The 1920s and 30s*

orphanage, first at Hartley and from 1933 on Durnford Street, where they remain to this day, caring for the elderly. The Sisters of St Anne were founded in 1911 at Vauxhall, South London, and in 1932 were invited by Bishop Barrett to establish a community in Wyndham Square under Mother Agnes Gordon-Smith.

The business of a bishop is not confined to the one city, however, and among Bishop Barrett's travels was a visit in 1932 to Buckfast Abbey for its consecration. The building of the Benedictine Abbey was a twentieth century testament to faith in much the same way as the building of the cathedral had been in the nineteenth. Started in 1882 and designed by F. A. Walters, the magnificent building was constructed entirely by the monks and in 1932 the 158 foot tower of Devon limestone had finally topped out. The celebrations (as one would expect from the Benedictines) were lavish and included the presentation of an episcopal ring to Bishop Barrett, while Cardinal Bourne attended as Papal Legate.

1939: Father Anton Boers, Chancellor of the Diocese of Plymouth and secretary to the bishop.

In 1933 Adolf Hitler was appointed to be Chancellor of Germany by a reluctant President Hindenburg. As the thirties progressed, the shadow of the little man from Braunau in Austria grew longer. *Krystalnacht*, and the subsequent, horrific persecution of the Jews, is rightly remembered, but less well known is the persecution of the Catholic Church in Germany and Austria. Pope Pius XI, who took a stand against Hitler, died on the eve of war in 1939. A High Mass was said at the cathedral by Rev A. Boers who, referring to the late pontiff's immense knowledge, said 'Learning is cherished by the Church, for it has enemies who must be attacked on their own ground.' These enemies would soon be attacking the cathedral itself.

Bernard C. Brien, KSG.

IN JANUARY 1933, the bishop conferred a Papal knighthood on Mr Bernard C. Brien, of The Elms, Stoke.

Mr Brien, a well-known city contractor, had been connected with Plymouth Cathedral for over fifty years.

Bernard was a great benefactor of the cathedral and was Master of Ceremonies. In 1926 he had received the Papal Cross *'pro ecclesia et pontifice'*. In a ceremony after High Mass, the bishop presented him with the brief and the declaration of the Order of St Gregory the Great, making him a Knight of St Gregory (KSG).

The 1920s and 30s — THE TWO WORLD WARS

Corpus Christi procession, 1935

MONSIGNOR Anthony Gilby has now retired and is living in Teignmouth but in the 1930s he was an altar server at the cathedral. *He writes...*

This photograph is of a Corpus Christi procession in 1935 or thereabouts. Just look at the crowds that would gather.

It shows the procession coming along Wyndham Street West on its way back to the cathedral for the third Benediction. The canon is Jeremiah Ryan, the administrator. I can be seen in the bottom right hand corner and my brother Peter is in the left hand corner. The bishop is Barrett.

The building on the left is Notre Dame Convent. Top left is the old Wesleyan Church which, by that time, had become the hall and gym of Notre Dame Convent School.

The procession would have started in the cathedral, passed through the garden into the convent grounds and stopped for Benediction. Then proceeded up Anstis Street where there would have been another altar and Benediction on the steps of the former Wesleyan Chapel and then back to the cathedral.

Look at the crowds, the street decorations and the flags and the girls strewing flowers!

From front, anticlockwise: The servers are Peter Cronin, Anthony Gilby, Frank May and Owen Routledge. Monsignor's brother Peter is the first face to be seen on the bottom left.

THE TWO WORLD WARS   *The 1920s and 30s*

The Chapter of Canons in 1938. Standing: Canons Denis Noonan, Jeremiah Ryan, Joseph O'Byrne, Isaac Cowd, John Lee. Seated: Walter Gaynor, John Joseph Higgins, Michael Burns (Provost) His Lordship Bishop John Barrett, Joseph Hurley, Monsignor Cyril Mahoney (Vicar General) and Jules Ketele. Inset: Canon Alan Power.

Pope Pius XI, 1922 - 1939

ON 10th February, 1939, Pope Pius XI died. A few days later, a Requiem Mass was celebrated in a packed Plymouth Cathedral. The prayer for the dead *'De Profundis'* was recited and after the High Mass the Dead March in 'Saul' was played.

Father A. Boers paid tribute to the late pope: "No pope in the history of the Church," he said, " has been so generous as Pope Pius XI in granting audiences to the faithful. Pigrims came from all parts of the world, and he was always willing to receive them."

Father Boers stressed two sides of the pope's character – his almost incredible capacity for work and his intensive devotion to the office and the task entrusted to him.

The 1920s and 30s   **THE TWO WORLD WARS**

His vast knowledge of almost all fields of learning and science marked him out in his early life as assistant to the head of the Ambrosian Library of Milan. "Learning is cherished by the Church," said Fr Boers, "for it has many enemies who must be attacked on their own ground."

The Holy Father's favourite recreation was the characteristically arduous one of mountain climbing and he proved his skill and endurance by being the first to climb Monte Rosa from the Italian (and hardest) side.

WORLD DISORDER

The seventeen years in which the pope ruled the universal Church coincided with a period in world history of confusion and disorder. His experiences as Nuncio in Poland made him aware of the evils of Communism and atheistic Bolshevism. He tried to prevent the confusion and horror of a Bolshevist domination of Spain, and he faced the persecution of the Catholic Church in Germany and Austria.

Fr Boers said the title the pope would have preferred for himself was 'Pope of the Missions'. His fostering care of the foreign missions was spiritually one of the most noteworthy features of his reign and the misery and disruption of missionary work in China during the Sino-Japanese war grieved him deeply at the end of his days.

"In praying for the soul of Pope Pius XI," added Fr Boers, "let us also pray that his successor in the World Church will reap the fruit of the work and prayers of the arduous life the late pope lived."

The cathedral filled with mourners for the late pope and (below) The body of Pius XI lying in state in St Peter's, Rome.

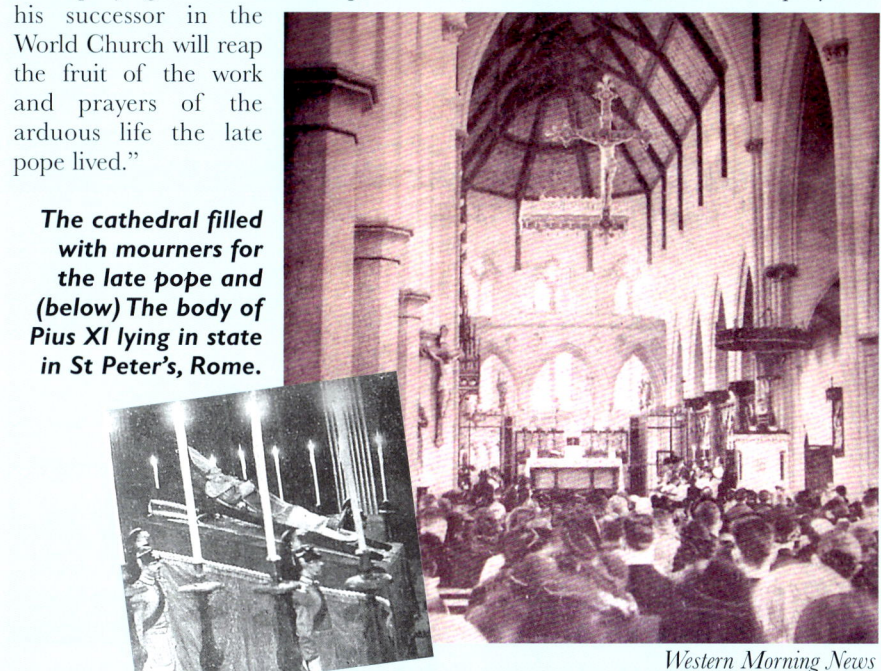

Western Morning News

THE TWO WORLD WARS *The 1920s and 30s*

This beautiful memorial to Bishop Keily has recently found a new home in the bishop's garden behind the cathedral.

The Second World War   **THE TWO WORLD WARS**

Chapter Six

MANY OF THE PHOTOGRAPHS of Plymouth during World War Two have achieved almost iconic status: two small boys, gas masks over their shoulders, standing amidst the rubble and watching a huge plume of smoke from the burning oil store at Turnchapel; a party of sailors clearing the remains of Millbay Station; and, most symbolically of all, the bombed out shells of St Andrew's and the Guildhall standing defiantly amid the ruination all around them.

In all the popular literature about the blitz, however, there seems to be a dearth of words and pictures about the Catholic population of Plymouth. Even Gerald Wasley's otherwise magnificent and exhaustive 'Plymouth, A Shattered City' contains no reference to the cathedral, its parishioners, priests and nuns. Perhaps, with death and destruction on such a massive scale (1,174 dead, thousands more injured, and tens of thousands of

1939: Plymouth city centre before World War Two and the blitz showing Saint Andrew's church and the Guildhall.

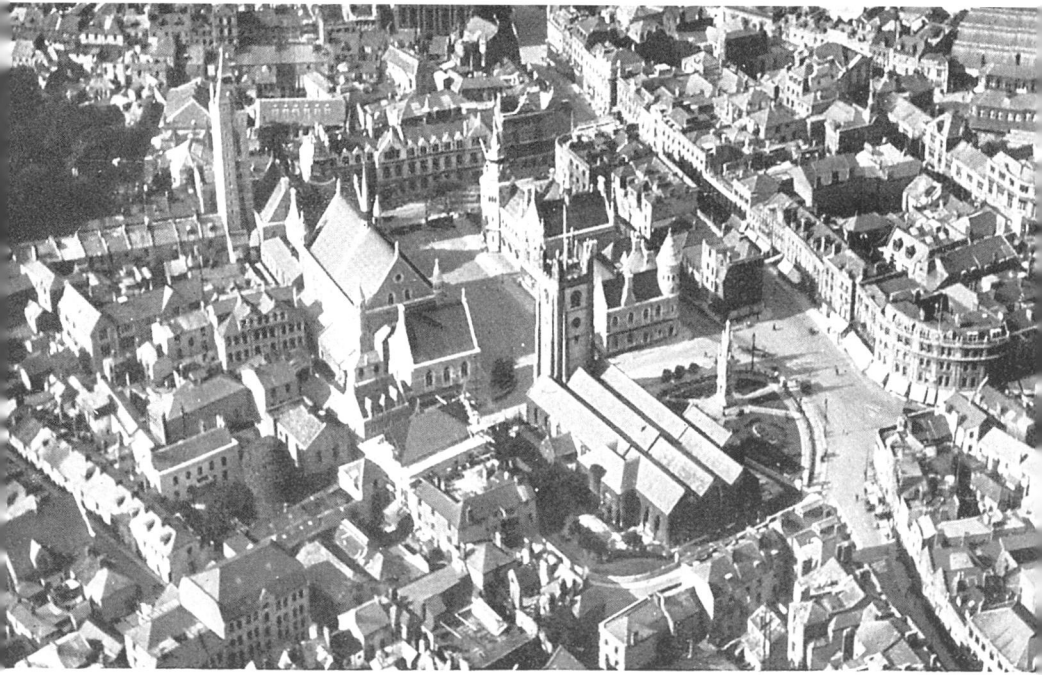

THE TWO WORLD WARS — *The Second World War*

properties destroyed), the missing out of one particular community was inevitable, but Plymouth's Catholics suffered with the rest of the population and made their own contribution to the war effort.

In 1939, with war on the horizon, the business of the Cathedral and the Diocese of Plymouth carried on as usual. On March 22nd there was a Pontifical High Mass at the Little Sisters of the Poor in Hartley to celebrate the Diamond Jubilee of Sister Raymund. The following day, Bishop Barrett was at Buckfast Abbey to install the Right Reverend Bruno Fehrenbacher as Abbot, the third incumbent of the post since the Abbey's re-founding. The Diocesan Record for 1939 also records the purchase of a site at Beaconfield, and expressed the hope that 'a new church will soon be built'. The intervention of one Adolf Hitler was to postpone this ambition until 1955, when the church of the Holy Family at Beacon Park would finally be consecrated.

Blessing at Buckfast, 1939

TIME magazine, Monday, Mar. 27, 1939

IN THE HILLS of Devon, in western England, some 30 years ago, 'Black Monks' of the Benedictine order undertook to rebuild Buckfast Abbey, crumbled to ruins in the 360-odd years since Henry VIII had dissolved England's monasteries. Laying up stone by stone under the direction of their German-born Lord Abbot, Dom Anscar Vonier, the Benedictines – never numbering more than a half-dozen at a time – labored for 25 years. Their abbey was consecrated in 1932, but the scaffolding on the great tower of Buckfast was not removed until last December.

A few days later death came to wise and kindly Abbot Vonier, 63. The Buckfast monks met together to elect a successor. Their choice was a German-born monk (now a British subject) named Dom Bruno Fehrenbacher *(right)*, who 28 years ago became a Benedictine upon hearing of the work in progress at Buckfast. Dom Bruno, at his election, was laboring at a task assigned him by the Abbot General – teaching Uniat (Eastern Catholic) Syrian priests in the Holy Land.

This week Buckfast expected 1,000 visitors for the Blessing of Lord Abbot Fehrenbacher by the Bishop of Plymouth. This rite, resembling a bishop's consecration, entitles the abbot – like a bishop – to preside at Mass, sit on a throne under a canopy, carry a crozier (crook) and wear a mitre.

The Second World War

THE TWO WORLD WARS

'Business as usual' was an illusion, of course, belied by what was going on all round. A Ministry of Health circular listed Plymouth as a neutral area, meaning that it would not be evacuated, a decision that was to have serious consequences for the whole South West. The term 'neutral' seemed to indicate safety, and as a result the population was swelled by people privately evacuating themselves from London. The local authorities realised that the city was likely to be a target, however, and had for some time been preparing civil defence. ARP volunteers were recruited, 2,500,000 sandbags were readied, and six miles of trenches dug. Air raid shelters were built, including one in the playground of the Convent School of Notre Dame, and, in May 1939, the first barrage balloons went up. The blackout was instituted on 1st September 1939, and two days later Neville Chamberlain made his famous radio broadcast announcing that the country was at war with Germany.

Air raid shelters were built, including one in the playground of the Convent School of Notre Dame.

Although the first few months of World War Two have often been described as the 'phoney war', it didn't feel like that for Plymouth. Just two weeks after the declaration of war, the Devonport based and crewed aircraft carrier HMS Courageous was sunk off Ireland by U-29. 515 men died; hundreds of Devonport families were plunged into mourning, and the priests and sisters of the Diocese had their first experience of comforting the bereaved – an experience that was to become all too common over the next six years.

1939: HMS Courageous had been converted to an aircraft carrier in 1928.

BELOW: The ship after being torpedoed.

'leet Air Arm Archive.

THE TWO WORLD WARS   *The Second World War*

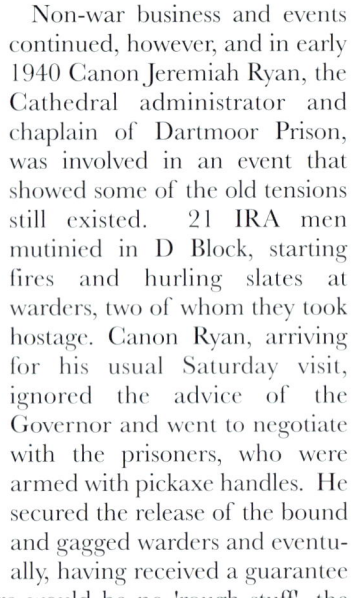

1940: Canon Ryan (right) found a mutiny in progress at Dartmoor Prison among IRA prisoners when making his usual Saturday visit.

> He secured the release of the bound and gagged warders ...and the mutineers surrendered.

Non-war business and events continued, however, and in early 1940 Canon Jeremiah Ryan, the Cathedral administrator and chaplain of Dartmoor Prison, was involved in an event that showed some of the old tensions still existed. 21 IRA men mutinied in D Block, starting fires and hurling slates at warders, two of whom they took hostage. Canon Ryan, arriving for his usual Saturday visit, ignored the advice of the Governor and went to negotiate with the prisoners, who were armed with pickaxe handles. He secured the release of the bound and gagged warders and eventually, having received a guarantee from the authorities that there would be no 'rough stuff', the mutineers surrendered. The drama made front-page news in the Daily Herald and Canon Ryan was hailed the hero of the hour.

Because of its proximity to the tempting target of the dockyard, the Cathedral and its environs were very much in the firing line during the blitz, and indeed the first major civilian losses of the war occurred in Stonehouse on 12th September 1940 when a fish and chip queue was hit by a bomb, and thirteen were killed.

The first half of 1941 saw some of the most intense raids suffered by any British city, beginning on 13th January, when 600 planes from Hitler's Luftwaffe pounded Plymouth with high explosive and incendiaries. From then on, the attacks were relentless, culminating in the great raids of 20-21st March, when 336 were killed and 20,000 properties destroyed or

The Second World War

THE TWO WORLD WARS

damaged. St Andrew's Church and the Guildhall were gutted, but the Cathedral suffered only minor damage. For the Convent of Notre Dame it was a different story, however.

Herbert C. Woodman, a parishioner and later historian of the Cathedral, who was manning ARP post 4B2 in the cellar of the Convent as the bombs fell, had an uncomfortably close view of the effects of incendiaries, and in particular a huge phosphorous bomb which fell on a grocer's shop at the junction of Cecil Street and Neswick Street:

'The shop just disintegrated into a huge inferno of fire. I knew I could render no help at this fire so I skirted it and went through a school door in Neswick Lane, into the playground, in which was built an underground shelter, capable of holding hundreds of people now sheltering from a rain of bombs and terror. I looked around this now very dark playground, in the

The cathedral had a narrow escape when the bombs destroyed Notre Dame Convent as well as the convent chapel and the former big Wesleyan church, used as the school hall and gym.

PLYMOUTH CATHEDRAL 1858-2008　　　　　　　　　　　　　　　55

THE TWO WORLD WARS

The Second World War

background lit up by searchlights and spluttering out incendiary bombs were the walls and the 205ft steeple. It was indeed a battle ground. Part of the school was on fire and near its entrance a group of people. There was Sister Mary, headmistress of the school. There was Miss M. Dustin, one of her teachers, and two wardens of 4B2, one of them a woman. Sister Mary was appealing to the male warden to go into her office and save the school registers and he replied it was impossible. I heard Sister Mary say "if you will not go, I will", and picking up her voluminous skirts she ran like a hare for the school entrance. She was almost to the door as I sprinted after and close to the open door when I caught her around the waist and hung on. She struggled and although we were in the thick of battle, because that was what this mighty air raid was, with its flash and roar of guns and exploding bombs lighting up this dark and uncanny playground, I felt as a Catholic I was committing sacrilege as my hands gripped her womanly waist.'

The registers were lost but the convent, though damaged, struggled on, until the next big raids in April delivered the coup de grace and also badly damaged the cathedral. A massive bomb, one of the biggest to fall on Plymouth during the war, fell at the junction of Cecil Street and Neswick Street, leaving a crater fifty feet across, which 'soon filled with water from a fractured water main and believe me, who saw it within minutes of it happening, it was big enough to float a fair size rowing boat'. A Catholic family called Riley were all killed when their house was demolished in the blast, and the roof, ceilings and windows of the cathedral were badly damaged, although the

The chapel of Notre Dame Convent next to the cathedral. The convent was totally destroyed in the air raids.

RIGHT: All that remained of the West Hoe pier after the blitz.
(Pen & Ink Publishing)

56   1858-2008 PLYMOUTH CATHEDRAL

The Second World War

THE TWO WORLD WARS

priests and nuns managed to save the Blessed Sacrament and sacred vessels.

At the convent, the school hall was the first to go, burned out by incendiaries, and then, at seven in the morning on 21st April, a huge time bomb exploded, devastating the chapel. The last Mass offered in the convent was said that day in the ruins, before the night's raids, which totally destroyed the convent, despite the efforts of the Sisters, some of whom climbed sixty foot ladders with buckets in a brave but ultimately futile attempt to put out the flames.

The following night brought the destruction of the church of the Holy Redeemer at Keyham, completely burned out in the inferno that engulfed Devonport when the dockyard was targeted by Dorniers and Heinkels. The church had been built not only to serve civilians but also Catholic sailors who had previously been worshipping on a hulk named the Monmouth moored in the Hamoaze and set aside by the Admiralty for the purpose. The foundation stone was laid on 10th April 1901; the church lasted almost precisely forty years.

Another Catholic casualty was Vescourt, the bishop's residence, destroyed by a land mine and forcing Bishop Barrett to spend the rest of the war with the Filles de la Croix at Stoodley Knowle Convent in Torquay.

The bishop was not alone in leaving the battered city; in that spring of 1941 as many as 50,000 people were leaving the city every night for the comparative safety of Dartmoor, Staddon

Plymouth city centre after the blitz. Saint Andrew's church is still standing but without a roof.

THE TWO WORLD WARS   *The Second World War*

Heights and Mount Edgecumbe, from where they had a grandstand view of the havoc wrought in the firestorms. Belatedly, in May 1941, the Government declared Plymouth an evacuation area and the exodus became more permanent. By the end of the war the population of the city was a mere 119,000, down from 210,000 at the outbreak of the war.

The pupils of the Convent of Notre Dame were sent to Camborne and Teignmouth, accompanied by some of the sisters. Other sisters remained behind, staying either in Plymouth or in Yelverton, from where they travelled back into the city to work with the many children who had not been evacuated. St Boniface's College at Beaconfield was also damaged in the April raids and the staff and some of the pupils were evacuated to Buckfast Abbey.

Pupils and staff of St Boniface's College were evacuated to Buckfast Abbey after the April 1941 air raids.

The Second World War

The role of both sisters and priests in bringing succour to the inhabitants of the devastated city was a vital one. There were not just the deaths and dismemberments to be dealt with; tens of thousands were homeless, and any infrastructure left undamaged by the Luftwaffe was hopelessly inadequate for the needs of the population. Water, gas and electricity were out of action for long periods, sewage flowed in the streets from wrecked sewers, 45 roads were completely blocked, and nobody was completely sure how many bodies were left in the rubble. Food was in desperately short supply, partly because of the destruction of stocks but also because of the disruption to transport; long queues formed merely at the rumour that bread was available. 'The spirit of the blitz' is a phrase often invoked to describe the attitude of the time, but the assumption that people chirpily went about their business with a smile and two fingers raised to Adolf ignores the grim psychological reality. Death was everywhere and just because you had survived the last raid did not mean you would get through the next. Fear haunted the city and many who had lost everything were in shock to the extent that signs had to be put up instructing where to go and what to do. The friendly and trusted face of a priest or sister who was undergoing the same deprivations as you were, and who moreover could provide support of the spiritual dimension, was a treasure beyond price.

Fear haunted the city and many who had lost everything were in shock.

George Street in the city centre, once a main shopping street, pictured after a heavy air raid in 1941.

THE TWO WORLD WARS *The Second World War*

The raids of April 1941 were the climax of the Luftwaffe's efforts to bomb the spirit out of Plymouth and thereafter the raids diminished, allowing Plymothians some time and space to recover.

A picture of the cathedral Chapter from 1946 has one notable absentee; Bishop Barrett did not, at the end of the war, return to Plymouth. Perhaps his responsibilities had taken their toll. Anyway, he was an old man: as one writer observed, 'the bishop who never grew up, grew old.'

'The bishop who never grew up, grew old...'

On November 2nd 1946 Sister Gertrude went to tell the bishop his lunch was ready, to find him dead in his chair with his breviary in his hand.

1946: Plymouth Cathedral Chapter in front of Bishop Barrett's portrait. Standing: Canons Isaac Cowd, George Cantell, Myles MacSweeney, Joseph O'Byrne, George Ford and Alan Power. Seated: Canons Jules Ketele, Cyril Mahoney, Michael Burns (Provost), Jeremiah Ryan and Walter Gaynor.

The Second World War   THE TWO WORLD WARS

St Boniface's evacuees, 1941

AMONG THE MANY happenings of those wartime days is a day which has become more special to me as the years have rolled by, *wrote Mr J. V. Isaacs in* **'The Link'** *the Plymouth Deanery Magazine.*. It is the day I went to Buckfast Abbey. No, not on a sightseeing trip, but as one of a small band of refugee college boys whose school at Beacon Park had become uninhabitable due to enemy action.

My memory fails to record the detail. Were we 60 or 80 strong? Was it a Monday or a Tuesday? Amongst a multitude of activity the mind's eye only captures images at random to record for the future.

Standing on the railway platform at Ashburton with masters and local officials sorting us out. The arrival at a butcher's shop and being shown to an upstairs room. The sheep's head brawn on the table (complete with remnants of wool still attached). The first day lecture by Brother MacDonald on being good ambassadors. The figure of a monk pushing a wheel barrow full of stone mason's tools and marvelling at the new glass panel door he had fitted by the following morning. The warm days cycling on roads then devoid of cars.

There is one memory which was captured not by the mind but the heart. It was the real Buckfast, the home of the monk, of prayer and of peace.

For it was to Buckfast we went to spend one of our last days before donning our uniforms. It was to Buckfast we went to give thanks on our return to 'Civvy Street'. In the years that followed, when things got a bit hectic, it was to Buckfast that we went to breathe once more the tranquillity and order, and find that peace which only the Lord can give.

Our thanks go to the few who are left who gave us sanctuary in those days, and to those no longer with us but who also played their part, our parents, the good people who opened their homes to us, and to the masters whose names still ring clear: Br. MacDonald, Br. Owens, Br. Grice.

1941 was a different world, even the Abbey wore a different face but the heart stays the same. I'm sure more talented minds than mine will be able to pen a more accurate account of the event, but before the memory fades, it's time for me to say *Thank You* to a school and an Abbey which helped so much in shaping my life.

St Boniface's College at Buckfast during World War II: Not a new school uniform, but the cast of 'The Mikado'.
(College History Dept.)

PLYMOUTH CATHEDRAL 1858-2008

THE TWO WORLD WARS *The Second World War*

Near the Sacristy door, in the south-east corner of the cathedral, is the traditional Pieta and Cross, which is used in the liturgy of Good Friday.

The Nineteen-Fifties   **THE POST-WAR ERA**

PART III ~ *The Post-war Era.*

Chapter Seven

THE STATISTICS of the Catholic Diocese of Plymouth in 1946 were very different from those described in the Bishop of Exeter's report of 1767. Then, there were a mere 12 Catholics, all of them identified by name; now the Catholic population was 33,500. There were 101 secular clergy and 80 regular, 60 convents, 72 schools, and 109 churches and chapels.

Bishop Francis Grimshaw, sixth Bishop of Plymouth.

This was the diocese to which Bishop Francis Grimshaw came in 1947. A Westcountry man – born in Bridgwater and educated at Prior Park College in Bath, he studied at the Gregorian College in Rome, before taking a curacy at Swindon. He was parish priest at Fishponds in Bristol and in Bath, and became Diocesan Inspector of Schools, a post coincidentally held by one of his predecessors, Bishop Keily.

Bishop Grimshaw was consecrated at the cathedral on 25th July by Archbishop Masterson of Birmingham. Following the consecration, there was a luncheon at which the Archbishop proposed the health of the new bishop and spoke of their long friendship, dating back to 1919 and Rome, when Bishop Grimshaw was still a teenager. In the evening, Bishop Grimshaw attended a reception for the laity in the field of St

THE POST-WAR ERA
The Nineteen-Fifties

Boniface's College in the company of several thousand people.

And so to work. The diocese may have been thriving, but it was not without its problems, and among the most significant of these was repairing the damage of war. The city was a scene of desolation, with many families homeless, bereaved or suffering the strain of nursing wounded or traumatised ex-servicemen and women; these were scars that would take years or even decades of pastoral and spiritual care to alleviate. Perhaps more immediately fixable was the fabric of the cathedral and churches. In this practical matter the bishop had something of a head start, for at the luncheon following his consecration, he had been able to announce that with his letter of congratulation Bishop Flynn had enclosed a cheque for £950, raised by the North to help restore the churches of Plymouth. This generous gift represented a much-needed kick-start for projects such as repairs to the cathedral roof and the complete reconstruction of the Church of the Holy Redeemer at Keyham.

1950: This informative programme booklet was produced for the centenary celebrations.

An early – and significant – event in Bishop Grimshaw's tenure was the conversion in 1948 of The Right Honourable Sir Henry Slesser, PC. A former Member of Parliament and Lord Justice of Appeal, Sir Henry was also a vice President of the Anglican Church Union and a member of the Anglican Canon Law Revision Committee. He was received into the church at Yelverton by Fr I Jones and confirmed the following day privately by Bishop Grimshaw. His conversion was described in the Catholic Times as the most important since that of Newman.

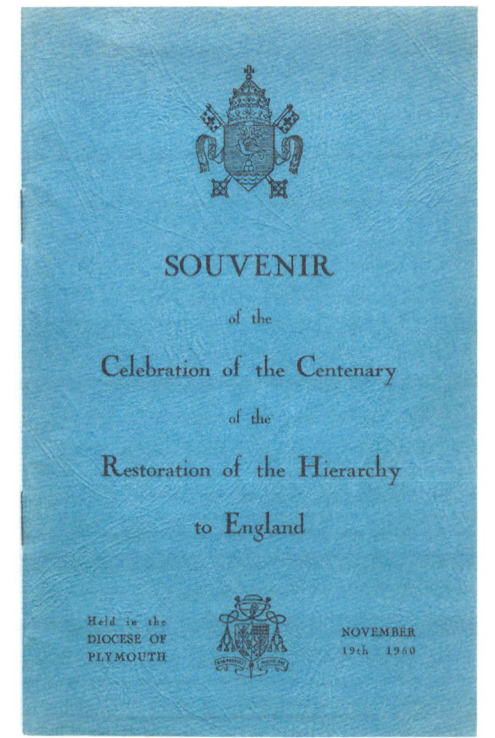

29th September 1950 saw further cause for celebration with the 100th anniversary of the Restoration of the Catholic Hierarchy. Local celebrations were delayed by the holding of the Centenary congress in London, but on 19th November there was a Pontifical High Mass in the cathedral, sung by Archbishop Masterson and with Bishop Grimshaw preach-

64   1858-2008 PLYMOUTH CATHEDRAL

The Nineteen-Fifties   THE POST-WAR ERA

ing. It was followed by a Grand Rally at the Palace Theatre with speeches from the archbishop, the bishop, Lady Eldon, Lord Clifford and P J Mowan.

Behind the headline events, there was the more mundane but no less important round of parish and diocesan affairs: marriages and masses, funerals and fetes, confirmations, meetings and socialising. Plymouth and its Catholic population were expanding and as a result the church of St Gregory the Great at Plymstock and the small brick church at Crownhill were made the centre for new parishes in 1948 and 1949 respectively.

Priests came and went, a notable departure being that in 1951 of the cathedral administrator Monsignor Jeremiah Ryan. Fr Ryan had been associated with the cathedral since 1924 and administrator since 1931, and had shown great courage in dealing with a prison mutiny at Princetown and extinguishing incendiary bombs dropped during the war. His successor was Canon George Cantell, whose energies would find their outlet in the restoration and repair of the cathedral. An engaging newspaper photograph from 1951 (right) shows the canon shortly after his appointment, chatting to a workman perched on scaffolding – one of many such chats he was to have over the next few years. The cathedral was not the only building to require attention and in 1950 the Church of the Holy Redeemer at Keyham was reopened and blessed by Bishop Grimshaw.

The new administrator of Plymouth Cathedral, Canon George Cantell—he succeeds Mgr. Canon Ryan, now at Weymouth—chats to a workman refacing the bomb-damaged fabric. Bishop Grimshaw on Sunday personally introduced the administrator to the parishioners. Canon Cantell, a convert, studied for the priesthood at the Beda College, Rome, and since his ordination has served at Penzance and Falmouth.

The cathedral Chapter celebrated its 100th Anniversary in November 1953 in recognition of which Cardinal Griffin,

THE POST-WAR ERA *The Nineteen-Fifties*

Archbishop of Westminster, visited the city. He received the Lord Mayor, Sir Clifford Tozer, at the Continental Hotel and the mayor returned the favour at the Mayor's Parlour. Cardinal Griffin spoke with admiration of the efforts being made to rehouse people and, after a High Mass, departed, leaving a gift of £3,000 towards the restoration of the cathedral.

Cardinal Bernard Griffin pictured in the library at Vescourt with Bishop Francis Grimshaw and the Chapter of Canons together with invited clergy and religious on the occasion of the Centenary of the Chapter.

The cathedral was in sore need of restoration; the most pressing repairs to the war-damaged fabric had been made and the building sported a brand new roof, but elsewhere the picture was grim. In a pastoral letter of 1954, Bishop Grimshaw described the state of things: 'Windows are broken, plaster is falling from the walls. My throne and the canons' stalls are in great need of renewal. We had some beautiful windows in the cathedral, including that of St Boniface ... But now the frames are warped. Most of them are filled with temporary glazing. The tiled floor is crumbling and the organ tells a trained ear of dust and debris still in its pipes. The whole fabric of the church is in urgent need of overhaul and restoration.' The bishop went on to announce an appeal for funds. The work would cost £20,000, 'a frightening figure in a diocese of this size', but the cardinal's gift had got things off to a good start and the Catenian Association had donated another £1,000.

The Nineteen-Fifties

THE POST-WAR ERA

The setting up of the appeal was one of Bishop Grimshaw's last duties, for in June 1954 it was announced that he had been appointed Archbishop of Birmingham following the death of Archbishop Masterson the previous year. Meanwhile, there was the small matter of the celebrations for the 1200th anniversary of the death of St Boniface. Anticipating a huge attendance, Bishop Grimshaw, the organising secretary, Fr Edward Carey, and the committee of fifteen had, in February, visited the only arena in the city capable of playing host to tens of thousands of visitors – Plymouth Argyle's ground at Home Park. Months of planning culminated, during the weekend of 19th-21st June, with what was probably the biggest event ever organised by the Diocese of Plymouth.

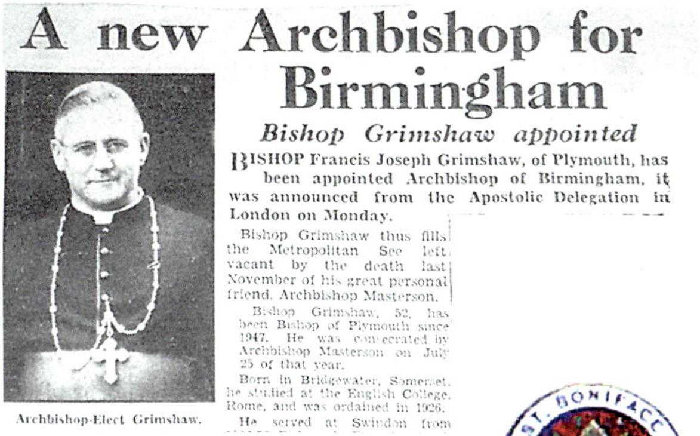

The list of prelates attending was impressive: three cardinals, three archbishops, and nineteen bishops. They came from all over Europe – Cologne, Munich, Utrecht, Ghent, Copenhagen, Paris, Quimper, Dromore, Kerry, Soli and Fulda – and domestically from Westminster, Cardiff, Edinburgh, Newcastle, Portsmouth, Lancaster, Nottingham, Munster, Shrewsbury, Brentwood, Clifton and Southwark. An international line up to celebrate a truly international saint.

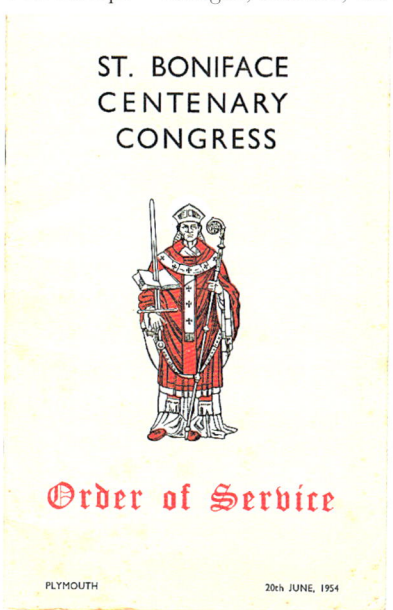

The list of prelates attending was impressive: three cardinals, three archbishops, and nineteen bishops.

Proceedings kicked off on the Saturday with a Pontifical High Mass at Buckfast Abbey, celebrated by Cardinal Frings, Archbishop of Cologne.

PLYMOUTH CATHEDRAL 1858-2008

67

THE POST-WAR ERA — The Nineteen-Fifties

1954: The view from the stands at Home Park as 12,000 watch the pageant of the life of Saint Boniface.

Here and there among the friendly people of Plymouth one caught a glimpse of a bishop's purple...

The next day was the great pageant at Home Park, written and produced by Alan Rye, Secretary of the Catholic Actors' Guild, and assisted by Rev James Peppard. Special buses were laid on to transport from the railway station the crowd of 12,000 who came to watch 200 actors enacted 12 scenes from the life of St Boniface, from his childhood in Crediton to his death at the hands of pagans in Friesia.

The Catholic Times described the hustle: 'It might have been any football crowd, pushing and milling its way through the entrance gates of the great stadium. But here and there among pushing, friendly people of Plymouth one caught a glimpse of a bishop's purple, or even the regal flash of a cardinal's red robes, as he made his way from his car, past the ice cream stalls, to his seat in the grandstand.' After the pageant, Cardinal Wendel, Archbishop of Munich, celebrated a Pontifical High Mass and the following day the prelates made a private visit to the shrine of another great Westcountry Catholic – that of the Blessed (now Saint) Cuthbert Mayne in Launceston. It was, all agreed, a splendid affair, and a fitting valedictory bow for Bishop Grimshaw, who was enthroned as Archbishop of Birmingham on September 14th.

The Nineteen-Fifties

THE POST-WAR ERA

Archbishop Grimshaw returned to Plymouth on June 14th 1955 to consecrate his successor, Rt Rev Mgr Cyril Restieaux, in front of a congregation that included priests from all over the diocese and a host of dignitaries including Group Captain Leonard Cheshire, VC, Admiral Sir Philip Enright, Sir Henry Slesser, Sir Colin Campbell, Deputy Town Clerk of the city, and the Chief Constable J F Skittery.

A native of Norwich, Bishop Restieaux studied at Ratcliffe College and the English College in Rome, and was ordained in Rome in 1932. On his return to Britain he was appointed to the staff of St Barnabas' Cathedral, Nottingham and became parish priest at Matlock in 1936. In 1948 he returned to Nottingham as cathedral administrator, where he soon became Vicar General and Provost of the Chapter.

The new bishop – at 45 the youngest in the country – had plenty on his plate. His first concern was the work of restoration of the cathedral. The original estimate of £20,000 had risen (surprise, surprise) to £30,000, and haste was needed to ensure that costs rose no further and also that the work was completed in time for the cathedral's centenary in 1958. Under the calm but watchful eye of Canon Cantell and the architect Mr Hugh Bankart, the work started just before Christmas. Over the next two years the floor of the sanctuary was re-laid with wooden blocks; all the plaster was stripped off and the old stone work treated; ceilings in the nave and transepts were replaced; consecration crosses of Portland stone were built into the walls; and the cathedral was rewired to allow for improved lighting and sound. Because of the expense, work on a new floor and heating and the refurbishment of the organ had to be delayed. The desired effect was one of simple dignity, and the new scheme of natural stone set against the sky blue of the ceiling achieved this triumphantly.

Bishop Cyril Restieaux, seventh Bishop of Plymouth and, below, his seal.

PLYMOUTH CATHEDRAL 1858-2008

THE POST-WAR ERA
The Nineteen-Fifties

1957 proved to be a busy year as the work of restoration and expansion continued: on 10th April, Bishop Restieaux consecrated the Church of the Holy Redeemer at Keyham, in front of 80 priests. Canon Walter Gaynor, parish priest at Keyham since 1924, had conferred upon him by the Pope the title of Domestic Prelate in honour of his long service under trying circumstances. New churches opened at Beacon Park, Exmouth, Chulmleigh, Wyke Regis and South Molton, and a new primary school at Whitleigh. The Carmelite Convent at Efford closed and the church was taken over by the diocese to become the parish of Efford under Fr Ian Jones. The same year also saw the publication of the first Diocesan Year Book, compiled by Canon O'Malley.

Solemn High Mass at the cathedral on 25th March 1958, sung by Canon Cantell and with a sermon from the bishop, had a special meaning for those (including 1,000 schoolchildren)

March 1957: An ordination at the cathedral during the renovation work.

The Nineteen-Fifties

THE POST-WAR ERA

attending as it marked the centenary of the cathedral. However, with the exact anniversary falling during Easter, priorities dictated that the full celebrations be a little delayed. A week of celebrations commenced on 27th April with High Mass, and on 1st May a Pontifical High Mass was sung by the bishop, and the sermon preached by Archbishop Grimshaw, who revealed again his fondness for Plymouth: 'Oh, it's good to be back again, even for a little while, in this city which recovered from her ordeal so completely and so well, and to see this building looking so lovely again. When the city's achievements are praised and are held up for emulation, as they have been recently in other parts of England, who could not feel a thrill of pride in the thought that he, too, for a time was privileged to be a citizen of this no mean city.'

At lunch after the Mass, Archbishop Grimshaw paid a special tribute to the two men most closely involved in the work of restoration, Mgr Canon Ryan and Canon Cantell, without whose unstinting efforts the cathedral had come successfully through a period of bricks and rubble.

As part of the centenary two Redemptorist Fathers, Rev George Lucas and Rev Dennis McCartan ran a Mission. 4th - 11th May was the Children's Mission, followed immediately by the grown-up version, which ran for another two weeks. With five Masses and a Mission Service on Sundays and three Masses and a Mission Service every weekday, it was a busy time for all involved.

May 1958: This prayer card was a memento of the Centenary Year Mission.

PLYMOUTH CATHEDRAL 1858-2008

71

THE POST-WAR ERA   *The Nineteen-Fifties*

1952: The new bell 'Peter' being hoisted up the spire. It was the gift of Fr John Haslip in memory of his mother.

In November Bishop Restieaux celebrated the silver jubilee of his ordination with a Pontifical High Mass at the cathedral, followed by a lunch for 200 at the Duke of Cornwall Hotel and an evening presentation at Devonport Guildhall, attended by (among others) the Lord Mayor. The bishop was presented with a cheque for 2,000 guineas, raised by donations from the diocese, a silver wallet inscribed with the names of four previous bishops, and a 'spiritual bouquet' from the children of the Diocese.

The fifties, a decade of restoration and growth, were drawing to a close. The cathedral was restored, new parishes had been created and churches built.

In the foreword to the 1960 Diocesan Year Book, Bishop Restieaux noted that 'in almost every parish, there has been a noteworthy attendance at Sunday Mass. This is proved by the parish statistics; and it is something for which we should thank God that even in our sparsely populated diocese signs of religious growth are not lacking. May this increase be much intensified during the coming year.'

The Chapel of the Sacred Heart in the North Transept.

Inset: The statue of St Anne in the niche to the right of the altar.

72   1858-2008 PLYMOUTH CATHEDRAL

The Nineteen-Fifties **THE POST-WAR ERA**

Rev Brother Edward I. Quinn

BISHOP RESTIEAUX is seen in this newspaper cutting presenting the pope's apostolic blessing on a parchment to Brother Edward Quinn of the Christian Brothers on the evening of 4th February 1958.

A dinner was held in the dining hall of St Boniface's College, Beacon Park, for Bro Quinn to celebrate his diamond jubilee as a Christian Brother. He had now retired from teaching after an active life of fifty years in the classroom.

Guests included the Abbot of Buckfast, the Rt Rev Dom Placid Hooper, the Rev Bro M. C. Wall, Brother Provincial, Prior Father C. White, Prior of St Mary's Abbey, Bodmin, Prior Father Alfaro, Prior of St Austin's Priory, Ivybridge, the Very Rev Monsignors Walter S. Gaynor and Michael O'Neill and the Rev Bro A. Grice, headmaster of St Boniface's College.

Many parist priests also attended. The bishop proposed the toast to Bro Quinn to whom, during the day, presentations had been made throughout the school on behalf of the staff and boys.

Before the dinner, a solemn Mass of thanksgiving was celebrated in the nearby Church of the Holy Family, presided over by Bishop Restieaux.

WEDNESDAY, FEBRUARY 5, 1958.

The Rev. Bro. Edward I. Quinn, celebrating his diamond jubilee as a Christian Brother, is presented with an Apostolic Blessing from the Pope by the Roman Catholic Bishop of Plymouth, the Rt. Rev. Mgr. Cyril Restieaux, at St. Boniface's College last night.

Bro Quinn was born in Dublin, receiving his early education in Christian Brothers' schools. He entered the Order himself in 1898 and taught in Ireland for 25 years. It was in 1924 that he came to England where he taught in colleges at Bristol, Liverpool, Great Crosby and Stoke on Trent.

He came to St Boniface's College in 1947 where, as for many years before, he specialised in art, manual crafts and particularly handwriting in junior classes.

Western Morning News

THE POST-WAR ERA *The Nineteen-Fifties*

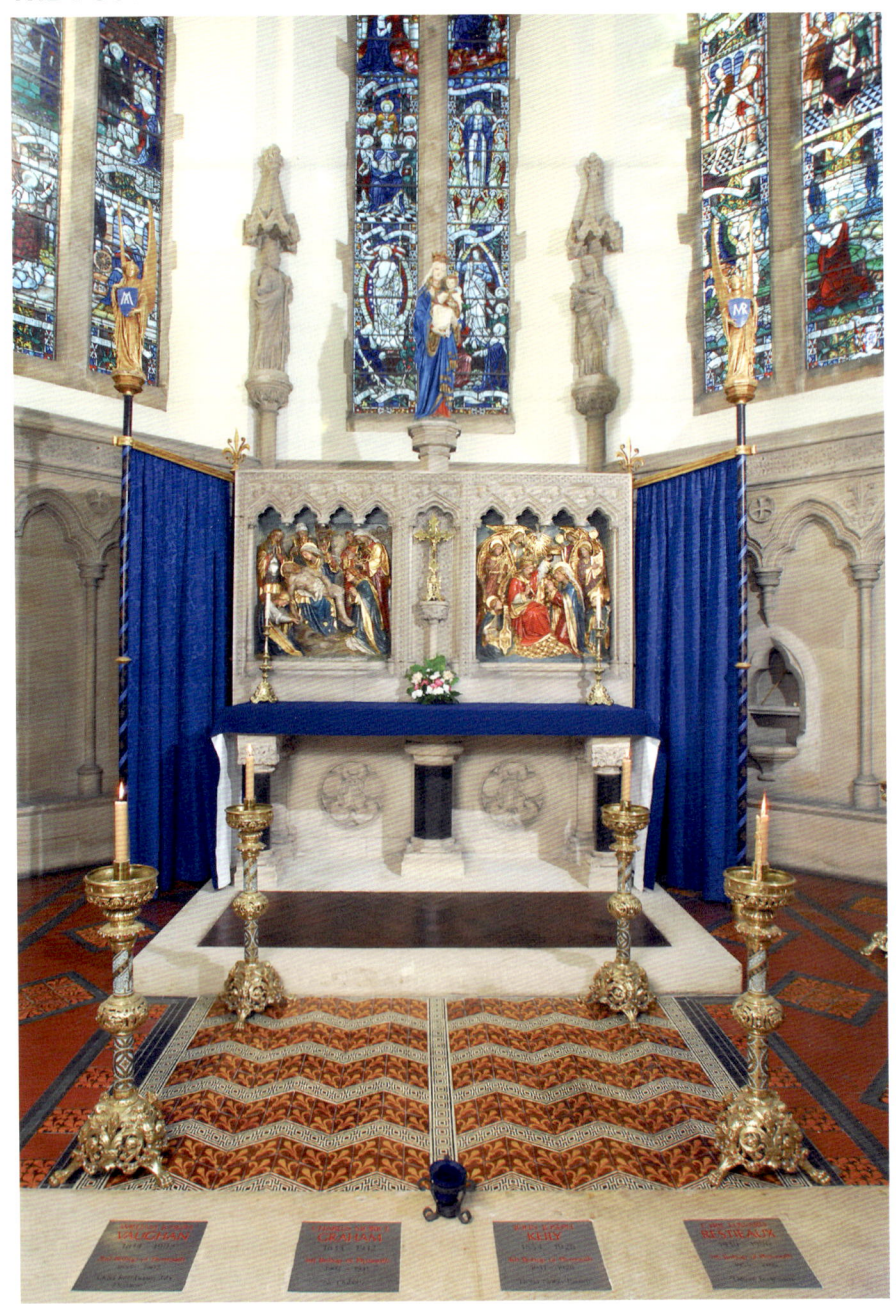

The Lady Chapel at the east end of the cathedral. The four plaques commemorate Bishops Vaughan, Keily, Graham and Restieaux whose bodies rest here.

The Sixties   THE POST-WAR ERA

Chapter Eight

PHILIP LARKIN famously asserted that the sixties began '…in 1963/ Between the Lady Chatterley trial/ And the Beatles' first LP'. Both events were emblematic of what was to be a decade of change; most noticeably for Catholics, perhaps, in the shape of the Second Vatican Council.

Change took place not only in the headlines, in the courts, in culture and in Rome, but closer to home; in Plymouth, the city centre rebuilding was in full swing, and the planned expansion of the suburbs would be seeing land, particularly to the north and east of the city, gobbled up for vast housing estates. Whitleigh, Southway, Estover, Leigham, Plymstock, Plympton — all would change immeasurably. The same was true in cities

Plymouth's Royal Parade at the heart of the city centre rebuilding programme.

THE POST-WAR ERA — The Sixties

and towns all over the diocese.

If these new housing developments were not to be mere soulless dormitories, however, they needed a heart, and shopping centres and like amenities could only provide for the more material needs.

The foreword to the 1960 Diocesan Year Book indicates that the Church was aware of this, mentioning the future building of churches in Plymstock, Efford, Plymouth City Centre and, further away, Newton Abbot, Whipton, and Branksome. At St Budeaux, the new primary school of St Paul's was nearing completion, and work was due to start in April on a new secondary modern in Torquay.

The Convent of Notre Dame was looking to the future, too, and also celebrating its centenary. After a sojourn at Teignmouth brought about by one A Hitler, the convent had returned to Plymouth, and temporary premises at Trenley, in Seymour Road, before moving to Alwin in Crownhill in 1955. Now there were plans for a new, purpose built Grammar School on the 13 acres of land adjacent to Alwin, and a facility for Catholic girls to equal that of St Boniface's for the boys.

From modest beginnings in 1852, under the patronage of Bishop Errington and the headship of a Mr Howe, St Boniface's College had become a thriving Grammar School; new science laboratories, form rooms, a kitchen, library and art room were added in the fifties and by the outset of the sixties the school had 485 boys on its roll. Over the years, St Boniface's had produced 50 pupils who had become priests and members

The new Notre Dame Convent and School, built on the site of Alwin and inset, Ashleigh in Teignmouth where the pupils lived from 1941 - 1945.

The Sixties

THE POST-WAR ERA

of religious orders, and the new decade continued this proud tradition when, on 25th February 1961 two more old boys, Rev Michael Cole and Rev Terence Fleming, were ordained in the cathedral by Bishop Restieaux.

At Plymstock, the building of the new church, dedicated to St Margaret Mary, was complete. The project had not been without its problems, particularly when the builders got into difficulties, but on 26th March Bishop Restieaux was able to open and bless the impressive new building. As one new church was opened, so work started on another – that of Jesus Christ the King on Armada Way. The site had been provided by the city, and a large slice of the building costs (over £50,000), was provided by an anonymous woman benefactor. The bishop laid the foundation stone on 17th September although, with work having started some time before, the shell of the building was already taking shape. The ceremony was well attended, apparently, and according to the Western Morning News 'They worshipped surrounded by stacked planks and steel scaffolding. They overflowed on to the gravelled approach, and in a solid mass across the street outside.' Inside, Bishop Restieaux blessed the stone, sprinkled it with holy water, and cut the sign of the cross on each side with a knife before the stone was lowered into place. In his address, the bishop noted that there were five churches under

The Revs. Michael Cole and Terence Fleming, former students of St. Boniface's College, Plymouth, were ordained by the Roman Catholic Bishop of Plymouth (Mgr. C. Restieaux) in the city's Roman Catholic Cathedral today. Above: The scene during the service.

1961: Bishop Restieaux ordains Fr Michael Cole and Fr Terry Fleming in the cathedral. Both are former pupils of St Boniface's College.

LEFT: Laying thefoundation stone at Christ the King in Armada Way.

PLYMOUTH CATHEDRAL 1858-2008

THE POST-WAR ERA *The Sixties*

The interior of the Church of Christ the King in Armada Way. It was the last church designed by Sir Giles Gilbert Scott and the gift of an anonymous lady.

The Sixties   THE POST-WAR ERA

construction in the diocese, and that this material progress was evidence of religious progress.

Church and school building were not the only areas in which the diocese was forging ahead. Pastoral care was receiving a boost in the shape of a new wing under construction at St Joseph's Home in Hartley. The Little Sisters of the Poor had first come to Plymouth in 1865 and opened a home for the aged in Stonehouse, and moved in 1882 to new premises in Hartley. Over the years the home had grown steadily and now provided care for 98 elderly residents; the new wing would raise the capacity to 118 and provide accommodation for extra Sisters who would come to St Joseph's after three years training at St Brigid's Novitiate at Dundrum near Dublin.

The Diocesan Year Book was by 1962 in its fifth year, and a great success. It now ran to over 200 pages and was supported in part by advertisements for Catholic business all over the diocese, from Seago's Chemists in Penzance to Richards' Garage in Wareham. Perusal of these adverts provides an interesting insight into how much things have changed in living memory. Telephone numbers have at most four digits, and in some cases

The Little Sisters of the Poor had first come to Plymouth in 1865 and opened a home for the aged at Stonehouse.

1960: Altar servers of the The Guild of St Stephen came from all over the diocese for their annual Mass.

THE POST-WAR ERA   *The Sixties*

> **Priests 'doing essential work among youth'**
>
> YOUNG Catholic priests were doing "absolutely essential" work among the youth of Plymouth, said the Very Rev. Canon G. Cantell, Administrator of the Plymouth Roman Catholic Cathedral, last night.
>
> He was proposing a toast to the Order of the Knights of St. Columba at the annual dinner of Council 94 (Plymouth) Knights, which was held in the Duke of Cornwall Hotel, Plymouth.
>
> There were a lot of stories these days of teenagers going wrong, but he wondered if they were as bad as all that. He urged parents to consult with priests more about their children.
>
> **VISIT TO ROME**
>
> He was sorry that there was not more enthusiasm among young Catholic men in Plymouth for the Knights.
>
> Mr. W. C. Hamilton, the Grand Knight, proposed the toast to the Queen and later the Bishop and

1962: Canon Cantell quoted in the Western Morning News after speaking at the annual dinner of Council 94 (Plymouth) of the Knights of St Columba.

only three or even two. Trades such as draper, bootmaker and fruiterer are common, and it is doubtful whether anyone has needed the services of a corsetière in a long time! Prices indicate a different age, too – bed and breakfast 16/6 (82½p for the post-decimalisation generation), or 23/– with evening meal. Less than fifty years ago, but a society that is almost unrecognisable today.

One thing that would be instantly recognisable, today or in any other age, is the oft-expressed concern about 'the youth of today'. In 1954 Bishop Grimshaw had expressed in the Evening Herald his worries about the attitude of some youngsters but laid the blame at the door of inadequate education. In the sixties, with a social revolution in full swing, the same old doubts were being raised more vociferously, but some took a more balanced view. Canon Cantell, speaking at the annual dinner of the Knights of St Columba in November 1962, said there were a lot of stories of teenagers going wrong, but he wondered if they were as bad as all that. The Canon went on to say that parents should consult more about their children with priests, and added that young Catholic priests were doing absolutely essential work among the youth of Plymouth. Ironically his comments, reported in the Western Morning News, come just above a separate article titled 'Youths Are Put On Probation'. Editorial mischief, perhaps?

At the cathedral, sufficient money had been raised to complete the last phase of post-war restoration. At a cost of £6,000 the old, rotten wooden floor was ripped up, an underfloor heat-

2008: The bishop's chair (cathedra) from which the cathedral gets its name.

The Sixties **THE POST-WAR ERA**

1966: The Chapter of Canons. Standing: Canons Anton Boers, John P. O'Malley, Adrian Chapple, Patrick O'Reilly, Kenneth Meiklem. Seated: Canons Joseph Elwell, Alan Power, Jeremiah Ryan, Patrick Tobin (Provost), Joseph O'Byrne, George Cantell, Robert Lyons.

ing system laid in concrete, and topped off with composition blocks in the nave and Derbyshire Spar in the north porch.

As the decade progressed, building continued unabated. £250,000 (£50,000 of which was provided by the diocese) was spent on the construction of Bishop Vaughan Secondary School at Manadon. Opened by the bishop on 16th March 1966, it immediately became the largest Catholic school in the diocese with a roll of 500, and replaced the existing secondary schools in the Cathedral and Keyham parishes. Under the headship of Mr John Cosgrove from St Mary's, its 21 staff taught GCE and CSE in a building 'replete with every modern facility'. There was provision to extend the school if and when necessary, and plans existed to become a comprehensive at a later date.

Bishop Vaughan Secondary School soon became the largest Catholic school in the diocese.

At Notre Dame, the long-awaited new buildings were finished (right), and opened by Bishop Restieaux on 26th September. The guest speaker was Peter Mason MBE, High Master of Manchester Grammar, who said: 'Education is neither secular nor purely intellectual, and a man can only come to terms with himself and the world he lives in if he learns the measure not only of his abilities but his limitations'. Given that he was opening a girls' school, Mr Mason's use of 'he' and 'his' might seem odd

THE POST-WAR ERA — *The Sixties*

to 21st century ears, but in the sixties political correctness was but a twinkle in the eyes of even the progressives.

The progressives were very much in the ascendant since the Second Vatican Council of 1962. The Council had been announced by Pope John XXIII in 1959, and three years of hard work were necessary before over 3,000 bishops assembled in the great basilica of St Peter's to debate the issues of the day. One of the major decisions was the approval of the document of the Liturgy, which was passed by the enormous margin of 2,102 votes to 11 and signalled the end of the Latin Mass.

In 1967 new schools were completed at Poole, Teignmouth, Bridport and Falmouth, and new churches at Brixham, Tiverton, Beaminster, Preston in Weymouth and Stoodley Knowle in Torquay.

As the new arrived, so departed some of the old. Canon Cantell retired as cathedral administrator in 1965 and was replaced by Canon Joseph Elwell. Mgr Canon Jeremiah Ryan retired as parish priest at Weymouth in 1967. He had been a faithful servant of the diocese for more than forty years, for nineteen of which he served as cathedral administrator. On his move to Weymouth in 1951 he became Dean of the Dorset Deanery, and served for 17 years at St Joseph's before retiring to his native Cork. Another departure was that of Canon Alan Power, priest of Bovey Tracey, who hung up his vestments on October 25th 1967 after 15 years at the parish. He was fondly remembered at the cathedral, where he served for six years, for his exceptional work with the choir, and he was both Treasurer and Precentor of the cathedral Chapter. Among ordinations

1962: The scene inside St Peter's, Rome as Pope Paul VI opens the Second Vatican Council.

The Sixties

THE POST-WAR ERA

was that of Fr Antony Cornish, a son of Launceston and another old boy of St Boniface's, where he was head boy in 1959-60. He was ordained in the cathedral by Bishop Restieaux on 17th September.

For some time, Bishop Restieaux had nursed the idea that a Catholic book shop would be an invaluable resource. With its central position, the new Church of Christ the King was an ideal location, and Rev Ian Jones, priest-in-charge, asked the Catholic Women's League if they would help. The Area Secretary Mrs B O'Leary took on the job with enthusiasm although, as she said, 'at this period my knowledge of books and repository work was NIL! In some desperation I ordered 85 rosaries and £10 worth of books and, for Christmas, 36 dozen Christmas cards.' By 1968 Mrs O'Leary was ordering cards by the 100 dozen and the bookshop was supplying parishes and convents with all manner of items. There were Catechetical, religious and educational books, books for the clergy, and books on Marriage Guidance. The Church of England became good customers, buying their altar missals and Sanctuary lights at the bookshop, and a sale or return service allowed parishes to stock stalls at their fêtes and bazaars. 'Other enquiries we receive from visitors range from the religious to the non-religious – in point of fact from baptisms to bus services!' All this was accomplished on a voluntary basis.

> 'In some desperation, I ordered 85 rosaries and £10 worth of books...'

1964: Bishop Restieaux pictured with all the children confirmed on Pentecost Sunday at the cathedral.

PLYMOUTH CATHEDRAL 1858-2008

83

THE POST-WAR ERA

The Sixties

Plymouth Catholic Choral Society was flourishing under the directorship of Fr Bede Davis, winning and then retaining the Cup in the Mixed Choir section at the Plymouth Festival of Music in 1964-5, and providing programmes of music all round the city. At Christmas there were Carols and Christmas Music at the cathedral, Mount Gould hospital, the Cheshire Home at Cann House, and St Joseph's Home. During Holy Week there were Masses sung at the cathedral and Our Lady of Lourdes, Plympton, and the Society were much in demand for celebrations of festivals such as that of the Blessed Cuthbert Mayne in Launceston. One of the staunchest members of the Cathedral Choral Society, and one of its founder members, was Mr Lalande Denley. In later years its accompanist and Secretary, he died in 1966, not long before the Society moved premises. For many years they had held their practices at Holy Cross School, but with the appointment of Fr Bede Davis to the cathedral, the choir moved there to practice in one of the larger rooms in Bishop's House.

Fr Bede Davis with his trademark accordion and, below, Canon Joseph O'Byrne.

In 1969 the Knights of St Columba celebrated their Golden Jubilee. The Plymouth Province organised a pilgrimage to Rome under the spiritual guidance of Fr Bede Davis, followed by a Mass celebrated by Bishop Restieaux and the Abbot of Buckfast at the Church of Our Lady Help of Christians and St Dennis at Marychurch, Torquay.

Another Golden Jubilee that year was that of Canon Joseph O'Byrne, parish priest at Holy Cross and Dean of Plymouth. Canon O'Byrne joined the diocese in 1921 and served at the cathedral, Falmouth, Sclerder, Blandford and Ilfracombe before moving to Holy Cross in 1937. Bishop Restieaux presided at the Solemn High Mass on April 9th, which was attended by the Lord Mayor and Lady Mayoress and priests from all over the diocese.

One of the well known families of the cathedral parish was the Pedricks. Their home was in Wyndham Square

The Sixties

THE POST-WAR ERA

and Miss F. M. (Flo) Pedrick, talking in later life, remembered family life affectionately: 'When I was a little girl my brothers would play at saying Mass at the top of the stairs. I, as a mere girl, had to take the part of the congregation – right at the bottom of the stairs!' Two of the brothers in question became priests: Dom Boniface Pedrick, OSB, Prior of Buckfast, and Fr Philip Pedrick parish priest of Stapehill, Dorset. Miss Pedrick herself was a long-serving member of the cathedral choir and went on to become deputy head of Notre Dame School and the National President of the British Federation of Notre Dame (de Namur) Associations.

Miss Florence Pedrick.

The sixties ended as they had begun, with developments in Catholic education. Plans were being drawn up for a new primary school at Estover, new classrooms were being built at St Budeaux, and construction of a new school to replace the old one in Camborne. The new school at Wool in Dorset had been running for a year and Our Lady's Primary School in Barnstaple for nine months.

Finally, and fittingly, there was the opening of the new Diocesan Shrine of St Boniface at Crediton. Bishop Restieaux blessed the foundation stone on August 2nd 1969 and returned in October for the opening. In his foreword to the 1970 Diocesan Year Book, the bishop wrote: 'May this new church be a real centre of interest and devotion, and also a place of pilgrimage where Catholics will go to honour our diocesan patron and pray for faith among the people of Devon, Cornwall and Dorset.'

The statue of St Boniface at Crediton in Devon – his birthplace.

PLYMOUTH CATHEDRAL 1858-2008

THE POST-WAR ERA   The Sixties

The Sisters of St Anne

THE CONGREGATION of the Sisters of St. Anne began in the crowded Vauxhall parish in South London in 1911, where a few devoted women helped poor people and their families, especially mothers and babies. A clinic with a hall was opened in 1914, and later a Refuge Hostel was begun where more than two thousand girls were provided for in the ten years of its existence.

The little band of workers became a diocesan religious congregation, with ecclesiastical approval, entitled the Sisters of St. Anne. In 1927 a special blessing for the Sisters and their work was received from Pope Pius XI and Solemn Approbation was later given by Pope Pius XII.

The Vauxhall large hall was the centre for grandmothers, mothers, children and babies, Girl Guides; and was also the first Catholic Maternity and Child Welfare Centre. In World War II the Sisters did 24-hour shift-duty at a Rest Centre during the bombing of London. Much of their own property was destroyed or damaged in the air-raids.

Their cancer hospital at Wimbledon was re-opened in 1948 as St Teresa's Maternity Hospital and in 1962 had over sixty beds. Now in 2008 it is a residential and nursing home for the elderly. Leper clinics were conducted at the Sisters' general hospital in Ghana, and much welfare work was done.

The Plymouth Convent *(below)* is just a short walk from the cathedral. It was opened in 1932 at the invitation of Bishop Barrett. The Sisters of St. Anne have worked with characteristic charity, patience and vigour in parishes in and around the City of Plymouth in peace and war. Indeed, no part of parish life is excluded from their activities.

The Latin motto of the Congregation is 'Sitio' ('I thirst') which summarises that zeal and charity which should animate Our Lord's servants. The Sisters' habit is blue-grey with a white collar, wimple and veil. It is simple and adapted for free movement in the world.

There is a wide scope for each Sister's work, because any previous career or experience can be made use of. The vocation of a Sister of St. Anne requires that she should be zealous for souls, and have a useful and cheerful temperament, above all that she should be 'trainable'. An ideal candidate for this active and modern Congregation of the Sisters of St. Anne.   **P.J.M.** *(1962 abridged)*

The Seventies   **THE POST-WAR ERA**

Chapter Nine

ANOTHER NEW DECADE, another new church. The little brick church built to serve the garrison at Crownhill and opened by Bishop Barrett in 1937 was now far too small to serve the growing population. Plans were drawn up by the architectural firm of Evans, Powell Associates and Bishop Restieaux laid the foundation stone in August 1969. Mr D Breen oversaw the construction and on 3rd September 1970 the new church was blessed by the bishop, who then concelebrated Mass with two former parish priests, Frs Michael McSweeney and M Joseph O'Brien. St Peter's is a building that looks firmly to the future; a bold, modernist statement, it remains a startling edifice nearly forty years on. In the same year the new chapel at the Convent of Notre Dame was opened, also by Bishop Restieaux.

1970: Saint Peter's church, Crownhill, inside and out.

In October 1970 Pope Paul VI announced the canonisation of the Forty Martyrs of England and Wales. One of their number was St Cuthbert Mayne, the first convert Anglican clergyman to die for the old faith. Educated at Bideford and Oxford, Mayne became rector of Huntshaw, near Bideford, in 1561. In 1573 he entered the English College at Douai and was ordained in 1575, upon which he returned to his native land at the manor house of Francis Tregian near Truro. He was arrested in 1577, imprisoned in the grim surroundings of Launceston Castle (known locally as Doomsdale and later the

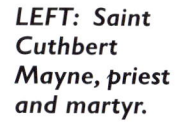

LEFT: Saint Cuthbert Mayne, priest and martyr.

PLYMOUTH CATHEDRAL 1858-2008

THE POST-WAR ERA

The Seventies

1970: Cardinal John Carmel Heenan was the guest of honour at St Boniface's College speech day.

'There are only two or three in a hundred million who can alter the course of history.'

temporary residence of another religious dissenter, the Quaker George Fox), found guilty at a mockery of a trial, and executed in Launceston market place on 30th November 1577. His body then suffered quartering, with the pieces being sent for display around Cornwall and his head exhibited at Launceston Castle. In 1921 an annual pilgrimage and procession was inaugurated to commemorate his martyrdom, and a portion of his skull, held at Lanherne Convent until its closure, was later encased in the cathedral altar.

For St Boniface's College, the annual speech day on 9th December 1970 was more than usually important, as the guest of honour was none other than Cardinal Heenan himself. He said to the boys: 'Never waste your time blaming the last generation . . . The fact is that in any generation there are only two or three in a hundred million who can influence the course of history. Most are what we are, and have to do their best in a limited sphere. You have to see what you can do about the limited part of the world in which you find yourself. Don't think you can change the world and make what is wrong come right. You can't. The place where you live and work is your world and what you can alter.' And to the parents: 'Don't be deluded that their education is being taken care of because they are at such a fine school. You are their prime educator.' Wise words. The school was doing well, with twenty or thirty boys each year (from a roll of around 430) leaving to pursue university degrees, and a shining record in sport, with five boys in 1970 playing rugby for Devon and two going on to play for England.

Elsewhere in education, the pace of development was unabated: extensions, new classrooms and whole new schools were planned or under way in Devonport, Exeter, Newton Abbot, Brixham, Torquay, Poole, Bodmin and Camborne, to name but a few.

Building work was not confined to schools: on 26th May 1971 Bishop Restieaux opened the new extension to the Plymouth Nazareth House Children's Home. With accommodation for

The Seventies

THE POST-WAR ERA

up to 28 children including babies, and for the staff, the extension was a thoroughly modern facility and the children were grouped into family units, each with their own Sister. The church of Christ the King required thousands of pounds spent on it after serious cracks were found in the walls; it closed in early 1973 but was open again after two years' work.

As ever, new developments were balanced by the passing of the old. Jack Pedrick died in 1970 after many years serving Mass at the cathedral and leading the Bishop's Own 14th Plymouth Scout Group. Mgr Jeremiah Ryan – Secretary to Bishop Barrett, cathedral administrator, a hero of the blitz and the Dartmoor Prison riots – passed on in his native Cork in November 1970, Canon Power in July 1971, and Canon O'Byrne, parish priest at Holy Cross for over 30 years, in 1972.

NAZARETH HOUSE VISITED BY PLYMOUTH'S CIVIC HEADS

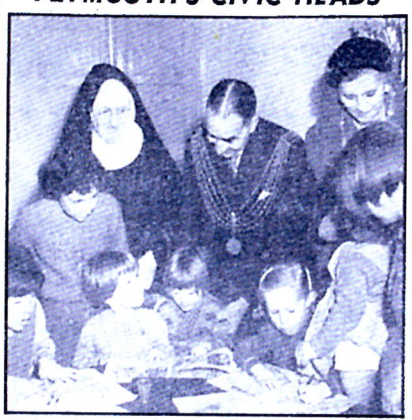

Paying an informal visit to Nazareth House today, the Lord Mayor and Lady Mayoress of Plymouth (Ald. and Mrs. G. J. Wingett) see some of the children busy with their colouring books. Left is the Rev. Mother Agnes.

Easter 1971 was a particularly joyous occasion for ten handicapped children and their helpers who made the first Plymouth Handicapped Children's Pilgrimage to Lourdes. Today the HCPT is a national charity but in 1971 the effort was more of a shoestring affair, with funds being raised through the collection, amongst other things, of Green Shield Stamps. The stamps are now lost in the mists of history, of course, as is 'old money', which took its bow in 1971. The Diocesan Yearbook of 1971 was the first to have a decimal price on its cover: 2/- or 10p.

Nazareth House Children's Home had been caring for orphans since the war. In 1958 the Lord Mayor and Lady Mayoress, Councillor and Mrs George Wingett, paid a visit.

1971: The first Plymouth Handicapped Children's pilgrimage to Lourdes which left from the parish of Our Lady of Lourdes, Plympton.

PLYMOUTH CATHEDRAL 1858-2008

THE POST-WAR ERA   *The Seventies*

The cathedral itself was undergoing changes, too. In 1972 the sanctuary was reconstructed to bring it into line with post-Vatican II and liturgical requirements. Most noticeably, the huge arched structure carrying the statue of Our Lady was removed, opening up the sanctuary, the old choir stalls were replaced, and a new forward facing altar built from Belgian black-fossil marble.

1972: The reconstructed sanctuary. The communion rails were retained.

The cathedral diary of 1974, compiled by the administrator Canon Elwell and published in the 1975 Yearbook, was 'intended to open the doors of the cathedral so that you can look inside and see some of the more important functions that have taken place there during the past twelve months.' It provides an insight into the yearly round: on the second Sunday in Advent, for example, the boys of St Thomas More's, East Allington, presented a Tableau of the Nativity with a Recital of Christmas Songs and Carols – a 'first-class performance', according to the newspapers. Christmas Night Mass was celebrated by His Lordship the Bishop; the Feast of the Epiphany coincided with World Peace Day and Mass was sung with specially chosen hymns to suit the dual purpose; on the fifth Sunday in Lent the Plymouth Philharmonic Choral Society gave a recital of Bach's Mass in B Minor; Maundy Thursday saw the Mass of the Holy Oils and the Priests of the Plymouth Deanery renewing their Priestly Vows, and the Easter Ceremonies concluded with Solemn Pontifical Benediction on Easter Sunday Evening. History all too often looks to the big events, the opening of new churches, installation of

The Seventies

THE POST-WAR ERA

bishops, anniversaries and pilgrimages, but the foundation of all these, without which nothing else has any relevance, is to be found in the Mass, the Baptisms, the confirmations and the unsung pastoral work of priests, sisters and laity.

Plymouth's Catholics had confirmation in 1974 of just how much their status had changed over the centuries when, on 1st April, Fred Johnson became the first Catholic Lord Mayor of the city since the Reformation. A native of the Barbican, a J. P. and member of Holy Cross parish, he appointed Fr David O'Driscoll of Holy Cross as his chaplain – another first. Also honoured, this time by the Vatican rather than Plymouth City Council, was Maurice Heron, altar server at the cathedral since 1927 and later Master of Ceremonies, who received the *Bene Merenti* medal. This medal is one of only two awarded by the Holy See to lay members of the church and was introduced by Pope Gregory XVI in 1834.

1974: Fred Johnson (L) was Plymouth's first Catholic Lord Mayor since the Reformation. Here, Bishop Restieaux presents him with a silver model of the cathedral.

Miscellaneous, but important events, 1974: the ten catechetical camps held around the diocese and organised by the Catholic Women's League were attended by 307 children; Canon Bede Davis reported that the Choral Society was in good health although he lamented the shortage of male members; and a special collection in the Plymouth and Torbay areas raised £508.08 for the Missionaries of Charity led by Mother Teresa of Calcutta.

Bishop Restieaux celebrated both his 65th birthday and 21 years as bishop in 1975. In those 21 years, 38 new churches had been built, along with new halls, presbyteries and schools. Perhaps more importantly, he had guided the ship with a steady hand through tricky waters, as Canon Elwell said in the Yearbook: 'In the changing times of the post-Vatican Council Church, our bishop steering a middle course, visiting every parish in Devon, Dorset and Cornwall at least once every three

'Our bishop,' writes Canon Elwell, 'has been an example of a devoted shepherd to his charge.'

THE POST-WAR ERA

The Seventies

years, urging his flock – priests and people – to be loyal and faithful, encouraging building, fostering change where necessary, untiring in his efforts to do what he feels right in the Church's interests, has been an example of a devoted shepherd to his charge.'

Brother Peter Schrode OSB died in August 1975. A gentle and unassuming man, he was the Master Mason for the construction of Buckfast Abbey. A native of Germany, he came to the Abbey in 1898 before leaving to serve his Mason's apprenticeship at the Abbey of En Calcat in France and returned to Buckfast in 1902 to begin work on the foundations of the Abbey, which was completed in 1938. Another to pass on was Canon George Cantell, who had so ably overseen the reconstruction of the cathedral after the war, and who died in September 1976.

Available for the sum of 25p in 1976 was the first cathedral guide booklet, containing a short history and 14 colour photographs. Another first in the same year was the performance of two 'Folk Masses' by students from Plymouth Polytechnic, who were joined by some of the cathedral youngsters to perform folk songs that were, to quote Canon Elwell, 'very beautiful indeed and quite inspiring.'

1976: The Church of Christ the King on the approach to Plymouth Hoe: one of the colour photos in the first cathedral guide book.

In the spring of that year, two years hard work culminated in the Mission to Plymouth. Titled 'Power for Life', the fortnight long mission involved Churches from all the denominations in the city: the focus for the Anglicans was at St Andrew's, and for the Methodists at Central Hall. On the Catholic side, the Redemptorists Fathers gave Missions simultaneously around the parishes, and there was an extensive programme of visiting and House Masses. The three Catholic Secondary Schools had their own Missions, and the fortnight culminated in an ecumenical rally at Home Park on Sunday 4th April.

The Seventies

THE POST-WAR ERA

The Queen celebrated her silver jubilee in 1977. There were street parties, concerts, and services of thanksgiving, all affected to some extent by the British summer which, having excelled itself in 1976, returned to its customary and rather damper form in 1977. For the Diocese of Plymouth, however, there was another cause for commemoration – the Fourth Centenary of the martyrdom of St Cuthbert Mayne.

As the first of the seminary priests to be martyred, St Cuthbert has always been an inspiration for British Catholics, and for those of the South West in particular. Celebrations opened with a Pontifical Mass on November 28th 1976 at the Catholic Church named for the Saint in Launceston. The following March, close on 1,000 people squashed into the Anglican church at St Cuthbert's birthplace of Sherwell, near Barnstaple, to hear Mass celebrated by Bishop Restieaux with a sermon preached by the Bishop of Clifton, Dr Mervyn Alexander. The climax of the celebrations took place at the end of June 1977, when the annual pilgrimage to Launceston took on a magnitude never before seen. The importance of the occasion was emphasised by the presence of Cardinal Basil Hume, making his first visit to the diocese.

The reliquary containing the skull of Saint Cuthbert Mayne. His head was rescued from a pike over the walls of Wadebridge by one of the Arundell family.

1977: Some of the crowd of 6,000 at Castle Green, Launceston for the fourth centenary of St Cuthbert Mayne's martyrdom.

PLYMOUTH CATHEDRAL 1858-2008

93

THE POST-WAR ERA

The Seventies

The Cardinal, Bishop Restieaux, and the 6,000 pilgrims who had gathered from all ends of the Diocese were welcomed on the Castle Green by the Mayor of Launceston Alan Buckingham, who spoke of the importance of people who stand firm by their beliefs. St Cuthbert's skull had been carried on foot by the Knights of St Columba from Golden Manor, and the Cardinal blessed the crowd with the relic before celebrating a Mass at which over 3,000 received communion — the largest number ever to do so on a single occasion in the Diocese. A fitting postscript to the celebrations took place on a cold November night when a small group of pilgrims heard Canon Adrian Chapple say Mass at Golden Manor in the very room in which St Cuthbert had celebrated his last Mass.

Cardinal Basil Hume at Buckfast on his first visit to the West Country with Bishop Restieaux (L) and Abbot Leo Smith OSB (R).

Also celebrating that year were the Sisters of St Anne in the cathedral parish, who marked their Golden Jubilee with a pilgrimage to the Shrine of St Anne at Auray in Brittany.

As the Seventies drew on into a twilight of unrest, strikes and economic problems, the lightning pace of development necessarily slowed. It is noticeable, for example, that where in the Sixties and early Seventies the Diocesan Yearbook would have two or three pages devoted to the building of new schools, by 1978 there were a mere four paragraphs dedicated to education, with no specific plans for building.

Detail from the Pike memorial window.

Indeed, concern is expressed about the growing rate of teacher redundancy, a direct result of the falling birth rate which itself was caused by more ready access to contraception and the legalisation of abortion.

1858-2008 PLYMOUTH CATHEDRAL

The Seventies

THE POST-WAR ERA

There were exceptions to the general air of belt-tightening, however. The new extension to the Church of Our Lady of Lourdes at Plympton, built at a cost of £12,000, was blessed by Bishop Restieaux at the beginning of 1976. At St Joseph's, Exmouth, Canon Haslehust opened a new classroom, kitchen servery and staff room, while St Joseph's House in Plymouth, once a home for the elderly, was converted at a cost of £50,000 to become a new house for the 85 boarders at St Boniface's School.

The sudden death of Pope Paul VI, after a reign of fifteen years, was announced on August 6th 1978. Among his many achievements was putting into effect the renewal of the Church voted for by the Second Vatican Council, and he was also the first Pope to visit Israel. His successor Pope John Paul reigned for only thirty-three days and was succeeded by Pope John Paul II.

Closer to home, Mrs Clare Rye died at the age of 90. She had

Mrs Clare Rye died aged 90. She had been a very generous benefactor of the diocese.

1978: Pope John Paul II who was elected when his predecessor died after only 33 days as the Holy Father.

PLYMOUTH CATHEDRAL 1858-2008

95

THE POST-WAR ERA
The Seventies

been a generous benefactor to the diocese. In 1951, she bought an Anglican church in Tavistock in memory of her husband, Mr Reginald Rye, who had died in 1945. This became the Catholic parish church of Our Lady of the Assumption (and St Mary Magdalene); and in 1961 she paid anonymously for the new church of Christ the King in Plymouth, which was designed by Sir Giles Gilbert Scott shortly before his death. Mrs Alicia O'Leary, a stalwart of the Catholic bookshop in Christ the King, received the *Bene Merenti* medal in 1978 in recognition of her long service.

1978: Over 800 young people attended the first diocesan youth rally at St Rita's Honiton on Whit Sunday.

A major development in looking to the future was taken in 1978 with the establishment of the Diocesan Youth Commission, with Fr Sean Flannery as Youth Officer. There had previously been no organised Catholic youth service in the Diocese but now, twice yearly meetings of the area representatives – a priest, teacher and youth worker from each of the eight areas – could organise and coordinate youth work through the Diocese. The first event to be organised was a Youth Rally at St Rita's Centre, Honiton, which was held on Whit Sunday and attended by over 800 young people.

The Seventies **THE POST-WAR ERA**

Another step in enabling young (and not-so-young) people to practice their faith was the establishment of a Catholic Royal Naval Chaplaincy at HMS Drake. This came under the umbrella of the Military Vicariate led by Bishop Walmsley, and the Chaplaincy itself was set up and run by Fr Paul Chamberlain, RN, who said: 'The whole purpose of the place is to be an open door – a sign of the Church's caring.'

Plymouth priests in Africa

AFTER 'blazing the trail' so effectively here in Kenya for Plymouth volunteer priests, Fr Con Twohig has now returned to his parish at Upper Parkstone in Dorset, *writes Fr Terry Fleming in the 1970 Diocesan Yearbook*.

In the short space of two years he accomplished much valuable work, including the building of the beautiful new church of St Boniface at Chebukaka. We look forward to welcoming Fr Seamus Flynn who will soon have to find his way around our 860 square miles of mountain and bush and get his tongue around the local Bantu language.

The parish is the size of a diocese. In fact it has as many maintained primary schools (27) as the whole Plymouth Diocese.

We offer Mass, preach the word of God and administer the sacraments in thirty scattered centres. One was recently started at Miendo and there were 225 attending and 29 infant baptisms.

Most people get a Mass safari only once a month and many not for two or three months.

One might hear between a hundred and two hundred confessions sitting in the cool shade of a tree and looking out over the rolling African countryside.

1970: Top: Fr Terry Fleming introduces Mishuku children to puppet, 'Fr Chad'. Below: Fr P. J. Kelly saying Mass during which children are baptised.

THE POST-WAR ERA — *The Seventies*

Fifteen years ago there was no road up Mount Elgon, an extinct (we hope!) volcano. In those days, Fr Stewart, the present parish priest, had to set off on foot through the tropical rain forest and return days later, having slept in mud huts.

The ordinary African is as delightful a person as you could wish to meet. He is consistently more polite, courteous and helpful than the average European. The children are most beautifully behaved and well-mannered. They sing and dance spontaneously and, when they overcome their shyness, their eyes sparkle and they have a charming smile. They have no toys but look after the younger children and herd their father's cows. They are all keen and avid for education.

Polygamy is still fairly commonplace and a great hardship for Catholic women forced into it. Yet if a marriage doesn't work out, the wife and children are not sent away, but the man builds another hut and takes a second wife. The marriage dowry in our tribe, the Babukusu, is presently 13 cows which does make for stability for if a wife ran off, her father would have to pay back the dowry! The marvel is that so many second and third wives still come to Mass although they are barred from the sacraments.

If our faith is to mean anything in practice, it must overflow into good works and an involvement in the social and economic development of the people we serve. This is an essential part of our witness to Christ. Therefore an 82 bed hospital has been established at Misikhu with a maternity wing, operating theatre and an out-patients clinic.

Our grateful thanks go to the people of the Plymouth Diocese who have helped with their prayers and generosity, such as by contributing to the salaries of our 34 catechists.

Father Terry Fleming is presently the parish priest in Plymstock and Fr P. J. Kelly was forced to leave Zimbabwe just a few years ago by Mugabe's henchmen. Other volunteer priests include Revv. John Bodley Scott, Gerard Gillespie, Larry Costello and Eddie Hayes.

Top: Baptisms while on safari.
Below: Catechist Philip preparing Catechumens for baptism beside the new church of St Boniface in Chebukaka.

The Eighties   **THE LAST THIRTY YEARS**

PART IV ~ *The Last Thirty Years.*

Chapter Ten

IN A PIECE in the 1980 Yearbook Monsignor Gilby, the Vicar General of the diocese, noted the main event of the year to come – Bishop Restieaux's Silver Jubilee – and went on to not only sum up the Bishop's achievements over those twenty five years but also the story of the diocese and the wider Catholic world: 'The twenty five years that have elapsed since the day of his consecration have been years full of activity and variety for the newly appointed bishop. He found a diocese well provided with priests, due in part to the large number of Irish priests, ex-servicemen and other late-vocations who had been ordained in the years immediately before his appointment. In our present circumstances it seems unbelievable that in 1953 there were eight priests ordained for the diocese, and in the following year, 1954, a further four priests. With numbers such as these it has been possible for the bishop to answer requests from outside the diocese for the help of priests in such work as education, the services, the Catholic Missionary Society and, most notably, the foreign missionary work of the Church in East Africa.

Monsignor Anthony Gilby was appointed Vicar General in 1975.

LEFT: Fiona Hutchings, former head girl of Stoodley Knowle **Convent School,** Torquay, was a volunteer teacher in **Africa in 1974. She is now** head teacher of Notre Dame **School.**

'Within the diocese the foundation work for a number of enterprises had already been laid in the immediate post-war years. Building on those founda-

PLYMOUTH CATHEDRAL 1858-2008

THE LAST THIRTY YEARS   *The Eighties*

tions the bishop was instrumental in helping forward the development of schools and churches and such work as the Catholic Women's League catechetical camps and vocations retreats. Through twenty five years the bishop has become a familiar and welcome figure at activities as diverse as a youth rally at Honiton and the Annual General Meeting of the Catholic Women's League when it has held its annual conference in the diocese.

'Side by side with the administrative work which is so much in the background, there are the many occasions during the year when the bishop is to be seen carrying out his duties in the parishes throughout the diocese. In normal times every parish has been visited once officially every three or four years. In addition the bishop shows himself ready to accept invitations to many gala occasions in the parishes up and down the diocese whenever that is possible.

'But without doubt, the major event in the twenty five years during which the bishop has cared for the diocese is the Second Vatican Council. This meant, of course, that the bishop, like bishops throughout the world, was absent from the diocese for a considerable period of each year during which the Council was in session – and all the greater the demands were made on the bishop while at home in the diocese. When the Council ended the bishops found themselves faced with the real work of putting into practice the decisions and insights of the Council. It is fair to say that there is no aspect of Catholic life which has not been affected in some way.

1978: Bishop Restieaux attended the AGM of the Catholic Women's League in Barnstaple.

'Bricks and mortar are not the only standard by which to judge the work of the bishop in the development of the diocese. Nor are they the most important. But it is of interest to note that in the course of twenty five years during which Bishop Restieaux has cared for the diocese there have been some 40 new churches or chapels built and opened. In some cases the new church has been built to replace an older building grown inadequate. In other cases a new church has been needed to provide for a shift in population. During the same period there has been, in addition, a steady development in the schools programme. More than a dozen new schools have been built.

In the course of twenty-five years...there have been some 40 new churches or chapels built and opened... and more than a dozen new schools...

The Eighties
THE LAST THIRTY YEARS

Many others have been extended. Once again, as with churches, the new buildings are sometimes erected to take the place of old buildings grown unsuitable for school purposes, or they are totally new foundations. Such church and school buildings are the necessary tools without which the Church cannot do its real work of building up the spiritual edifice. It is the bishop's task to oversee the provision of these necessary things while at the same time keeping clearly before us the spiritual building of the Church.'

Wednesday April 9th was a beautiful day for Bishop Restieaux's silver jubilee. The needle of the cathedral spire was sharp against the spring sky. At 12 noon the clergy in choir dress, accompanied by representatives of the religious communities of the diocese, processed through the cathedral, followed by 70 clerics in identical chasubles. Bringing up the rear were the Archbishop of Southwark, four other visiting bishops and Bishop Restieaux, and behind them Cardinal Basil Hume, Archbishop of Westminster. The concelebrated Mass was followed by a buffet lunch in the Great Hall of Plymouth Polytechnic attended by 470 priests, nuns and representatives from every parish. Mr Tony Sutton, diocesan solicitor, spoke for the laity and revealed that contributions to the Jubilee Fund totalled £25,000 which the bishop wished to be devoted to the

Cardinal Hume (centre) with Bishop Restieaux on his right and the Archbishop of Southwark on his left, together with the four other bishops who concelebrated Bishop Restieaux's silver jubilee Mass.

PLYMOUTH CATHEDRAL 1858-2008

THE LAST THIRTY YEARS　　　　　*The Eighties*

The Chapter of Canons in 1980 at the time of Bishop Restieaux's silver jubilee. Standing (L-R): Canons David O'Driscoll, Desmond Haslehurst, Michael Kennedy, Walter Costello, Michael Walsh. Seated (L-R): Canons Kenneth Meiklem, Joseph Elwell, Mgr Anthony Gilby, His Lordship the Bishop, Canons Adrian Chapple, Francis Balment and Francis Gallagher.

The centenary of the consecration of the cathedral was celebrated with a Mass featured on television and an interview with Bishop Restieaux.

welfare of children in the diocese. Canon Kenneth Meiklem, speaking for the Chapter and clergy, described Bishop Restieaux as a '…hopeful, holy man, who can smile', and had 'shrewdness in selecting his helpers, an instinct for the problems that are important, and the ability to trust others.'

There were other anniversaries to celebrate that year. In June nearly 4,000 Catholics attended Mass at Exeter Cathedral to celebrate the 13th centenary of the birth of St Boniface. Among their number were 55 pilgrims from Haar, near Munich, with their parish priest, Fr Xaver Gröppmair. There were also pilgrims from Hamburg, Tauberbischhofsheim, Paderborn, Whitechapel and Tooting. September 22nd was the centenary of the consecration of the cathedral, celebrated with a concelebrated Mass that was covered by Westward Television, who included an interview with Bishop Restieaux and four special programmes in their 'Faith for Life' epilogue series.

The Eighties   **THE LAST THIRTY YEARS**

Another big event was the National Pastoral Congress, held in Liverpool and attended by over 2,000 delegates including 33 representatives form the Diocese of Plymouth. The occasion was a great success, according to (then) Fr Bart Nannery: 'It was a magnificent and confident response from the Church in England and Wales to the call of the Second Vatican Council and to the invitation of our bishops. If the final outcome proves equally successful in its own way there will be no need for another, at least of this kind, for many years to come.'

Change was afoot at the cathedral, with Canon Elwell stepping down after 15 years as administrator to take charge at the church of Christ the King in the city centre, replacing the recently retired Canon Hann, who had been in charge since 1971. Canon Hann's retirement was to last only a year and he died in November 1981. Canon Elwell's successor as cathedral administrator was Canon Bede Davis who was also on the Religious Advisory Board of Westward TV and its successor Television South West. The board met every six weeks to plan the religious output of the station, foremost among which was the 'Faith for Life' programmes which went out at the end of broadcasting every day, and were seen by up to 80,000 viewers. Live transmission allowed for topicality, but the change of franchise gave rise to changes that were on the whole beneficial; Thursday was no longer 'Catholic Day', for instance, but now contributors might be given two or three days in a row to develop a theme, although pre-recording meant current issues were harder to address.

1980: Canon Bede Davis becomes the new cathedral administrator.

The fortunes of the Navy continued to affect Plymouth and its Catholics. Straitened economic times meant that the Dockyard's workforce had shrunk enormously from its peak of 35,000 in the fifties and this, combined with the knock-on effect in support industries, was leading to a slowing down in

The Royal Naval Dockyard in Devonport from the air.

PLYMOUTH CATHEDRAL 1858-2008

THE LAST THIRTY YEARS
The Eighties

1982: Marines from Plymouth were among those fighting in the Falklands War. (Picture courtesy of The Royal British Legion)

the growth of the Catholic population which would actually turn into a decrease with the 'Peace Dividend' of the late eighties and early nineties. The Falklands War of 1982 brought back, for an older generation, memories of World War Two, with local Marines fighting and dying at Bluff Cove, Goose Green and Tumbledown, while at sea two Plymouth ships – HMS Antelope and HMS Ardent – were lost. Priests and sisters were once again comforting bereaved families.

The early eighties does seem to have been a time of anniversaries: Sister Josephine of the Sisters of St Anne celebrated her Golden Jubilee in 1980, and Keyham Barton Primary School 75 years of Catholic education in 1981 – three quarters of a century during which the Sisters of Charity of St Paul had served the school selflessly and, incidentally, nurtured nine vocations for the priesthood. Holy Cross Church on Beaumont Road celebrated its centenary in the same year. Bishop Restieaux attained the golden jubilee of his ordination in 1982 a few months after the Sisters of St Anne celebrated the golden jubilee of their arrival in the cathedral parish. In between the bishop and the sisters, Buckfast Abbey passed its centenary with a Mass of Thanksgiving at which Cardinal Hume presided.

The Sisters of Saint Anne come to the cathedral altar rails for a blessing for their 1982 golden jubilee.

The Eighties

THE LAST THIRTY YEARS

For St Boniface's College, 1983 was a year of farewells, particularly to the old college buildings at Beacon Park, which were demolished to make way for a housing estate called, appropriately, St Boniface's Park. Two masters retired: Mr William Flint, head of English, after thirty years, and Frank Hannon, art master, after twenty nine. Other schools, too, bade goodbye to long-serving teachers in the form of Miss Sheila Featherstone (St Boniface's Primary) Miss Shanahan (Notre Dame Prep) and Mrs Gwen Pengelly (Notre Dame High). In 1981 Notre Dame had gone comprehensive, a move very much in the tradition of the foundress of the Sisters of Notre Dame, St Julie Billiart, who believed that a good education should be free and available to all who wished it.

William Flint, retired from St Boniface's after 30 years.

William Flint, teacher.

WILLIAM FLINT taught English at St Boniface's College for thirty years. Writing in 1983, in one of the first issues of *The Link*, the new Plymouth Deanery magazine, he bids the school farewell...

"During my early days, I held the Christian Brothers in great awe and never ceased to marvel at their dedication and talents. It has also been my privilege to work with an army of lay colleagues and especially those who worked with me on stage. I remember one of them, flat on his back holding up the 'walls of Jerusalem' on opening night because a bolt had worked loose from the scenery!

"Countless boys live in my mind and there were some great ones. Perhaps the bishop might be interested in how some of his priests spent their youth. Although in my first year Father Terry Fleming slipped through the net, drama and the school play nonetheless provided the thread.

"After his quite brilliant sound effects for 'Journey's End' (my first production) Fr Peter Webb did not know whether to go for the stage or the Church! Following his delightfully coy *Nicole* in 'The Prodigious Snob', Fr Adrian Toffollo's moving *St Bernard* seems to have prepared the way. It was intriguing (and I never type-cast) to watch Fr Anthony Cornish's brooding *Judas* in 'Caesar's Friend'. Fr Robert Plant (bishop please note) revelled in a particularly nasty venomous creature, *Wossup the Terrible* in 'John Willie and the Bee People' and I shall never forget Fr John Deeny's shy and gentle *Dragon* in 'Trudi and the Minstrel'.

"St Boniface's, Beacon Park, was my home and I still have great affection for it."

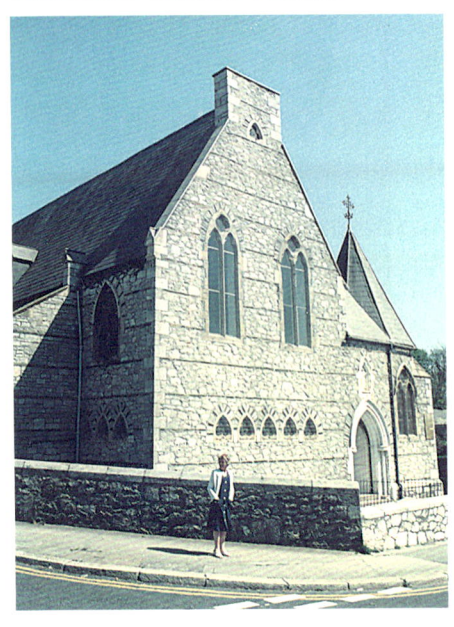

THE LAST THIRTY YEARS

The Eighties

At the cathedral an appeal was under way to raise £4,000 for repairs to the spire. £820 was raised at the Summer Fete, enough to pay for the erection of ladders and some essential re-pointing. The Church of St Michael and St Joseph, out on a limb at Mutton Cove, however, had reached the stage where the cost of repairs was too high. Parish priest Fr Bart Nannery said 'Naturally people will miss the old church, for many it has been part and parcel of their lives. But after much consultation and debate it was unanimously decided that the only solution was to sell it to a developer and build a new church, presbytery and hall in the centre of the parish. The church, designed (as was the cathedral) by Joseph Hansom, was the oldest in the city, having been consecrated in 1861 by Bishop Vaughan. The final Mass was celebrated by Bishop Restieaux on Ascension Thursday 1984 and two weeks later the much loved church was demolished to make way for 48 luxury flats.

The original church of St Michael and St Joseph, Mutton Cove, Devonport.

Its replacement, St Joseph's, was designed by Christopher Bilson and Peter Reading, and opened in November 1985 with a Mass celebrated by Bishop Restieaux and attended by, among others, the Lord Mayor, Janet Foulkes MP, and the Anglican Bishop of Plymouth Kenneth Newing. Another man present that day, probably allowing himself a quiet smile, was Fr Charles Foley, for whom the moment represented the fulfilment of a long-held dream. As parish priest at St Michael and St Joseph in the sixties, Fr Foley had fought a losing battle with the gradual disintegration of the church fabric and this, combined with the church's isolation,

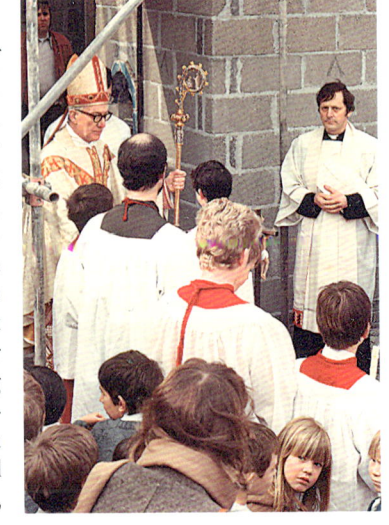

RIGHT: Bishop Restieaux and parish priest Father Bart Nannery (R) at the laying of the foundation stone for the new St Joseph's church.

1858-2008 PLYMOUTH CATHEDRAL

The Eighties

THE LAST THIRTY YEARS

convinced him that a radical solution was needed. The site of the old Raglan Barracks in Stonehouse was being disposed of by the Ministry of Defence. Three and a half acres of prime land was a target for other denominations and commercial interests alike but, undaunted, Fr Foley decided that the site was just what he wanted, not only for a church, but also sheltered housing and a school. Canon Desmond Haslehust, at that time in charge of education, had other priorities, as did Bishop Restieaux, and fellow priests subjected Fr Foley to frequent ribbings on the golf course over his apparent *folie de grandeur*. Lacking allies and with official policy focused elsewhere, Fr Foley decided to bypass the usual channels and headed off to London to visit the department responsible for the reallocation of MoD land, where the official with whom he met was an old parishioner from his days at Teignmouth.

As parish priest, Fr Foley had intervened to help the man's son secure a school place, and the official was only too happy to return the favour. Fr Foley returned to Plymouth with first refusal on the prized site at the knockdown price of £11,000, a *fait accompli* which the powers that be were in no position to ignore. Funds were released to buy the site and build a school, which was opened in 1968. Fr Foley moved in 1973 to Ilfracombe, out of mischief's way, but returned for the opening of the new church of St Joseph. In 1990 the development of the site was completed

Father Charles Foley was subjected to frequent ribbings on the golf course about his long-held dream for a new church.

The modern design of St Joseph's combined old features with the new.

THE LAST THIRTY YEARS — The Eighties

The sheltered housing of St Therese's Court is next to the new Devonport church.

RIGHT: In one of his last acts before his retirement, Bishop Restieaux consecrated the new church of St Joseph.

with the opening of the sheltered housing of St Therese's Court.

Bishop Restieaux was now 75 and decided that, after thirty years as bishop, it was time to hang up his mitre. His successor, announced on November 19th, was to be Mgr Hugh Christopher Budd, the 48 year old administrator at Brentwood Cathedral. Educated at St Mary's, Hornchurch, the Salesian College, Chertsey, Cotton College, Grove Park and the English College in Rome, and he was ordained in 1962 by Cardinal Heard. A varied career ensued: tutor in theology at the English College; lecturer in theology at Newman College; Head of Training at the Catholic Marriage Advisory Council; and Rector of St John's Seminary in Wonersh. David John, then a student for the priesthood at Wonersh, remembered the new bishop in the December 1985 edition of *The Link*, the Plymouth Deanery magazine: 'He is a very kind and caring man ... Though his full name is Hugh Christopher Budd, he refers to himself as Chris Budd. He is a solid figure, though not overweight. I remember him once cooking bubble and squeak by the ton for us for breakfast! On the activities front he enjoys hill walking and is "crazy" about cricket.'

The Eighties
THE LAST THIRTY YEARS

Bishop Restieaux said his farewells with two Masses – one celebrated with the priests of the diocese on December 17th and the other, a people's farewell Mass, on January 11th 1986. Bishop Budd's enthronement and consecration took place on 15th January at a ceremony attended by 700 people, of whom 160 were priests and 21 bishops. The Lord Mayor, Chief Constable, Flag Officer and Port Admiral attended, as did the Anglican Bishops of Exeter, Truro and Plymouth. The homily was given by Cardinal Hume and the principal celebrant was Bishop Restieaux. Bishop Budd spoke of 'the marvellous gift I have received through prayer and the laying on of hands – the gift of episcopal ministry for service in the Church of Plymouth. I feel a great joy, a certain trepidation and a hope that my ministry among you will be fruitful.'

> **'I feel a great joy, a certain trepidation and a hope that my ministry among you will be fruitful.'**
>
> ✠ **Bishop Christopher Budd.**

The diocese inherited by Bishop Christopher reflected Plymouth's wider society in that it had to meet the challenges of an ever more rapidly changing world. Gone were a lot of the old certainties such as the idea of a job for life, as witnessed by the ever shrinking dockyard workforce. Council houses were being sold off, and the responsibility for social housing was being taken up by the as yet untried housing associations, and the spectre of HIV/AIDS was taking up an increasing amount of column inches in the press. The City of London – all red braces, Porsches and fat bonuses – was flourishing, and the economy stronger than it had been for decades, but in the far south-west the much heralded trickle-down effect appeared, to your average Plymothian, to have dried up altogether.

Bishop Christopher Budd, the eighth Bishop of Plymouth.

Changing times or not, the business of the diocese continued. Some events were headline news; mostly, people carried on doing their bit. Miss Florence Pedrick, of the cathedral parish, was elected one of four Catholic Women of the year, in recognition of her 18 years on the National Board of Catholic Women and her long service at Notre Dame High School. Another stalwart of Notre Dame, English teacher May Power, died in 1989. Father

PLYMOUTH CATHEDRAL 1858-2008   109

THE LAST THIRTY YEARS   *The Eighties*

Michael Lock left the cathedral in October 1986 to become parish priest at Camborne, reducing the number of priests at the cathedral to two. Kathleen Mary Wilcocks, first chairman of the CWL in Plymouth, died at Nazareth House. In 1987 Canon Elwell celebrated the golden jubilee of his priesthood. Brother Sreenan retired as headmaster at St Boniface's in the summer, to be succeeded by Brother David Kavanagh.

Christians Together in Plymouth held the first big Whit Sunday Festival on the Hoe; Bishop Budd celebrated the silver jubilee of his priesthood by concelebrating Mass with some 50 other priests; the City Mission of 1988 attracted a huge turnout to Mass in the Guildhall. Canon Richardson, the Dean, departed to become parish priest at St Joseph's in Branksome; Sister Mary Peter of St Anne's Convent celebrated the golden jubilee of her profession; John Edmund Kewell died; the Diocesan Commission for Justice and Peace was launched and the painted wrought iron work around the Blessed Sacrament chapel was beautifully restored to its former glory.

As the eighties drew to their close, statistics revealed that the Catholic Church in England and Wales numbered 4,100,000. A single parent on benefits received £115.48 weekly; 48% of people thought they were richer and 36% poorer and 48% more unhappy. Margaret Thatcher's hitherto apparently unsinkable ship appeared to be springing a few planks; and the Berlin Wall came down. What next?

John Kewell died in 1989. He was tireless in his work with the Diocesan Vigil Group, which he had helped to found 29 years earlier.

1988: Plymouth Guildhall was packed for the thanksgiving Mass at the end of the City Mission.

The Eighties   **THE LAST THIRTY YEARS**

St Joseph's, Devonport.

THE ORIGINAL church of St Michael and St Joseph in Mutton Cove, Devonport closed its doors for the last time after the final Mass on Ascension Day, 31st May 1984. The church was built in 1861 and the architect was Joseph Hansom, famous for his design of the Hansom cab, who had recently completed Plymouth Cathedral. Kathleen Manahan McEvoy was over from the USA visiting her family and her old parish: "On that evening, Bishop Cyril Restieaux celebrated the final Mass, after more than 120 years of worship.

"Canon Michael Kennedy, former parish priest and Canon Walter Costello were concelebrants. Several other priests attended the Mass including Dom Philip Manahan OSB from Buckfast Abbey, Fr Danny Longland and Fr Bart Nannery, the present parish priest.

" The church was 'bulging at the seams' and it afforded me great pleasure to see so many familiar faces."

Two weeks later, *wrote Father Nannery*, the church was razed to the ground to make way for 48 luxury flats. Originally built to seat 800, it had become too large for the present congregation and much too costly to repair. With the extension of the Dockyard and all the development in the area, after being so badly bombed during the war, the church had become isolated from the people.

In its time, St Joseph's had produced more priests and nuns than any parish in the diocese including Bishop Cotter, former Bishop of Portsmouth, seventeen priests and twenty Sisters.

The original decorated interior and high altar of the old church of Saint Michael and Saint Joseph.

RIGHT: These three uncles of Cardinal Cormac Murphy O'Connor were once curates at St Joseph's, Mutton Cove.

PLYMOUTH CATHEDRAL 1858-2008   111

THE LAST THIRTY YEARS　　　　　　　　　　　　　　　　*The Eighties*

St Joseph's, Devonport.

One well-known parish family was the Wiltshires. Celia Porter (née Wiltshire) wrote in *The Link*: 'My twin sister Josephine (Jo) and I, and later on my younger sister Mary, attended St Joseph's school, next to the church, from the age of six. This was way back in the early 1930's when there were no school dinners or free milk. We brought sandwiches or pasties for lunch and were given an enamel mug of hot cocoa. I can remember the taste was more enamel than cocoa! Then we brought our halfpenny each day for a bottle of milk, the creamiest milk, the like of which I've never tasted since.

'I have vivid memories of the concerts in the school hall, and the ceilidhs with my mother pounding away at the old piano and Canon Power fiddling for dear life on his violin. This was of course during the second World War when St Joseph's became a house from home for the many American servicemen before they went to Europe.'

Pat Wilton (née Walsh) writes: 'My mother and father were married at St Michael & St Joseph's and later my sister Eileen were baptised, made our First Confessions and Holy Communions there, and were confirmed. Both she and I were married at the church too. In the 1930s money was very scarce and the housing was poor. When war was declared, we had to go to Devonport Guildhall to be measured for gas masks. When the blitz started in earnest, we were evacuated to Camborne in Cornwall from Devonport railway station.'

From the top: The twins Jo and Celia Wiltshire in 1928, Pat Walsh and her sister in 1933 and below, the hard-working parish council of St Joseph's pictured with parish priest, Fr Nannery in their new church hall.

The Decade of Evangelism **THE LAST THIRTY YEARS**

Chapter Eleven

1990 SAW THE INVASION of Kuwait by Saddam Hussein's forces and the departure of Margaret Thatcher as prime minister. Change was afoot at the cathedral, too; after 32 years in the Plymouth Deanery, ten of them as administrator, Canon Bede Davis was leaving to become parish priest in Falmouth, taking his boat but not Molly the cat with him. As well as his administrative duties, Canon Bede Davis had been chairman of the Deanery Communications Committee and it was at his suggestion that the Deanery magazine *The Link* had been set up in 1983. His successor, announced in the summer, was to be Fr Bart Nannery from St Joseph's in Devonport.

1990: Oil wells ablaze in Kuwait.

The Nineties had been declared the Decade of Evangelism, but the world's attention was diverted somewhat from the official start in December 1990 of this initiative by the spectre of war in the Gulf. The build up of forces had been gathering momentum for months and by the beginning of 1991 war was only a step away. Dick Birch, of the Diocesan Justice and Peace Comm-ission, wrote a piece on the prospect of war for *The Link*, in which he quoted Pope John Paul II's Christmas message: 'The demands of humanity living today ask us to move resolutely towards the absolute banning of war and to cultivate peace as the supreme good, to which all policies and strategies must be subordinated. Before this God who is offered to man, this

'War cannot be an adequate means for the solution of international problems . . . it never has been and never will be.'

Pope John Paul II

LEFT: The Peace Chapel in Plymouth Cathedral.

THE LAST THIRTY YEARS — The Decade of Evangelism

God who is disarmed, we must also lay down our arms. War cannot be an adequate means for the solution of international problems . . . it never has been and never will be.' Also quoted was a joint statement by Cardinal Hume and the Archbishop of Canterbury: 'In our view if armed force has to be used by the international community to oust Saddam Hussein from Kuwait, it will be a tragedy and could easily become a human, environmental and political disaster. We must all hope and pray that the war will be swift with as few casualties as possible.' In the event the war was brief and casualties, at least on the Allied side, blessedly few, though up to 100,000 Iraqis and Kuwaitis perished.

Bishop Restieaux celebrated his 80th birthday in February 1990.

In January 1990 Bishop Christopher celebrated the fourth anniversary of his consecration and the following month Bishop Restieaux celebrated his 80th birthday. With Bishop Restieaux's retirement, the focus of diocesan development had shifted; Bishop Christopher wanted to make the cathedral the centre of his ministry and to this end was keen to move from the bishop's mansion to the cathedral.

Steeplejacks Tina and Ian Dawson high above the city on Plymouth Cathedral spire.

1858-2008 PLYMOUTH CATHEDRAL

The Decade of Evangelism   THE LAST THIRTY YEARS

Vescourt had been home to Plymouth's bishops for over sixty years. Quite palatial, with its walled garden, grand rooms and domestic staff, Vescourt represented an older, grander and arguably more privileged era. But before Bishop Budd could move back to the original Bishop's House, it was going to need a little attention. The fine old Grade II* listed building was suffering from years of neglect; in particular, the top floor was almost derelict and now played home to a flock of pigeons. Where once there had been a thriving community of six priests, now only two rattled around the sad old building with its peeling paint, damp, and flaking plaster.

The cathedral, too, was looking a bit the worse for wear. Since Canon Cantell's efforts in the fifties, work had been carried out piecemeal, and while the fabric of the building was in reasonable shape, the layout harked back to a pre-Vatican II era with the altar far away at the east end and isolated from the congregation. Bishop Budd's vision for the re-ordering of the cathedral was to make it into a space where Mass was more inclusive, less removed, a little less 'us and them', if you like. In addition, the primary school next door was divided between two sites, with two classrooms on the site of the old St Mary's Secondary Modern. The old Notre Dame Convent School site was completely derelict, with weeds and even trees taking over.

Bishop Budd's vision for the re-ordering of the cathedral was to make it into a space where Mass was more inclusive.

The demands of Cathedral House, the cathedral itself, of the school, and the need for some sort of social provision in the form of sheltered housing all coalesced. While it was obvious that the three acres of the cathedral site could satisfy everybody's needs, the complexities of the project were equally obvious. It was to be perhaps the biggest project undertaken by the diocese since the cathedral was built, but where to start?

Plans for the three acres of the cathedral site included 84 houses and flats.

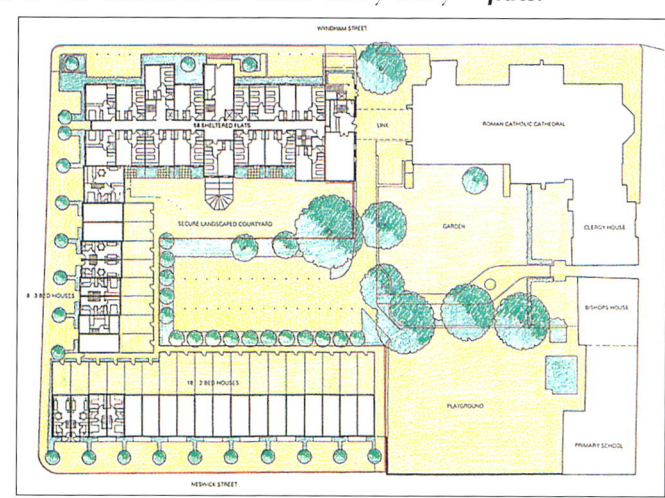

Funding was the major hurdle; the work on the cathedral, Cathedral House and the

PLYMOUTH CATHEDRAL 1858-2008

THE LAST THIRTY YEARS   *The Decade of Evangelism*

proposed Cathedral Centre would cost upwards of £2 million, which could only be raised by leasing or selling some of the adjacent land. However, nobody would be interested while the two primary classrooms were smack bang in the way, so further money was needed to get over that hurdle. Fr Nannery got out his contact book. Architect Keith Proctor suggested as a potential partner for the social housing Sovereign Housing, who were keen to gain a foothold in Plymouth. Dame Janet Fookes MP gave unsparingly of her time, using her knowledge of the Westminster machine to badger the Department of Education. The City Council became involved as the scheme developed into one of the largest and most complex renewal projects Plymouth had seen since the post-war redevelopment.

Dame Janet Fookes MP was made a Life Peer, Baroness Fookes, in 1997.

The web of needs, timescales and conflicting interests was a complex one and there were hundreds of hours of delicate negotiations. Fr Nannery phoned, talked, cajoled while Bishop Christopher inspired and supported, both men secure in the belief that God would help them navigate these tricky waters, and gradually a partnership emerged, one that was later described in *Housing and Planning Review*: 'The Partnership was the vital and only way forward. The miracle is that it gelled together with funding from various agencies simultaneously … Partners included the Roman Catholic Cathedral Trustees, Plymouth City Council, Sovereign Housing Association, the Housing Corporation, the Department of Education, English

New houses on Anstis Street were among the first to be occupied.

The Decade of Evangelism   **THE LAST THIRTY YEARS**

Heritage, the European Union and the Churches National Housing Coalition. RJG Partnerships coordinated the work of three architectural practices: Harrison Sutton, for the cathedral and cathedral offices, Wilks and Vaughan for the school, and Keith Proctor for the social housing.'

Notre Dame House provides sheltered housing on the site of the former Notre Dame Convent School.

The total cost was in the region of £5 million, raised in a variety of ways. There were grants from the DoE, English Heritage, the EU and other bodies, a leasing agreement with Sovereign Housing, and the proceeds of the sale of Vescourt, which became a drug rehabilitation unit.

Remarkably, the whole process was accomplished in only three years, and the end result was a complete makeover for the area. There were 84 new homes for social housing and

THE LAST THIRTY YEARS

The Decade of Evangelism

the elderly, with the cathedral having rights of nomination. The school, for 120 pupils, provided a modern educational environment and a new playground. The local conservation area was extended and the link between Wyndham Street and Wyndham Square repaved and relit. In the centre of the complex, the bishop's garden provided the 'green lungs' of the project, and the new car park was secure and vandal-proof. The new, secure entrance lobby of the cathedral linked through to the Cathedral Centre, built as part of the deal by Sovereign Housing at a cost of £1 million and incorporating into its structure part of the old Notre Dame walls.

The residents' private courtyard at the rear of Notre Dame House.

In Cathedral House, the pigeons had gone. A lift was installed, along with new heating and electrics, the offices were completely revamped, and the accommodation improved. The bishop, Fr Nannery, resident priests and visitors could all now enjoy dry, draught-free and airy rooms. In the Chapter Room, with its glorious vaulted ceiling, the old partitions were ripped out. In short, everything received the attention for which it had

1995: Cardinal Basil Hume at the official opening.

1858-2008 PLYMOUTH CATHEDRAL

The Decade of Evangelism

THE LAST THIRTY YEARS

been crying out, and this was all accomplished without compromising Cathedral House's status as a listed building. Thus, all the old woodwork was retained, maintaining the building's unique atmosphere, while it turned out that the original main staircase was something of an engineering masterpiece, cantilevered out from the walls without visible means of support, and is included in the American School of Architecture's curriculum.

In the cathedral itself the new high altar, made from granite and provided by the Chapter, was sited at the centre of things and included in its structure a relic of St Boniface and St Cuthbert Mayne, thus providing a link with the past. The ambo was moved to the west end, and the parish of Shaldon provided this new 'table of the Word'. These and many other alterations resulted in a simple, elegant and warm interior, more inclusive and reflecting Bishop Christopher's wish that the Gospel message must be relevant for the age.

The new altar situated at the centre of the nave and transepts.
INSET: The reliquary containing relics of St Boniface and St Cuthbert Mayne.

One of the side effects of the re-ordering was that the Diocesan archives, until now housed in the basement at Vescourt, were homeless. Fr Chris Smith, the diocesan archivist, cleared some unused rooms at the Priest's House in Dartmouth and several tons of boxes, files and paper were re-housed. The archives have now found a permanent home at Buckfast Abbey, and a new archivist, Sister Benignus of Stoodley Knowle Convent.

On 17th May 1995, with all the work completed in the nick of time, Bishop Budd and Fr (now Canon) Nannery met Cardinal Hume and his Secretary at the

LEFT: The Ambo, the 'table of the Word' at the west end.

PLYMOUTH CATHEDRAL 1858-2008

THE LAST THIRTY YEARS   *The Decade of Evangelism*

CONSECRATION OF THE ALTAR 1995

Clockwise from top: Bishop Budd anoints the altar; Prayer over the Gifts; Cardinal Hume's homily; Cementing the saints' relics into the altar.

1858-2008 PLYMOUTH CATHEDRAL

The Decade of Evangelism **THE LAST THIRTY YEARS**

station for what was to be a momentous day. The Cardinal visited the Cathedral School, and then opened the Cathedral Housing Complex (Notre Dame House) before presiding at the Mass of the Consecration of the Altar, attended by over 750 people including the Archbishop of Fulda. Bishop Budd performed the actual consecration using a 'lavish amount of Oil of Chrism', assisted by Vicar General Mgr Anthony Gilby and Canon Nannery.

An evening buffet, prepared by Sister Maureen Lomax and the catering staff of Notre Dame School, was enjoyed by all and then… 'The Cardinal, after a long day and a weak cup of tea, finally retired for the night. His secretary had something slightly stronger because he said it would make him sleep! Next morning at breakfast the cardinal, asked did he sleep well, said "No." His secretary's comment displayed a complete lack of sympathy: "It's your own fault, you should have taken my advice on the nightcap – I slept like a log."

The final accolade for the project came the following year when it was joint winner of the national prize in the NHTPC National Partnership awards. *Housing and Planning Review* said: 'This is a happy occasion where the whole is much greater than the sum of the parts, all the more worthy of celebration when it is remembered that this is in St Peter's Ward, which was recently cited as the most deprived council ward in Britain.' In fact, it was at St Peter's Anglican church in neighbouring Wyndham Square that Mass was celebrated while the work inside the cathedral was in progress; thanks to the vicar, Prebendary Sam Philpott.

While all this frenetic activity was taking place, the life of the cathedral continued, despite having to dodge around the builders and deal with the dust, noise and intermittent interruptions to the electricity supply that are a part of every building

(L-R) Canon Nannery, Cardinal Hume and Bishop Budd on the way to the Cathedral School and NotreDame House.

The Notre Dame Housing scheme won a national partnership award in 1996.

PLYMOUTH CATHEDRAL 1858-2008

THE LAST THIRTY YEARS *The Decade of Evangelism*

project. There was the business of attending to the needs of a thriving diocese: Masses to be said, baptisms carried out, and fêtes, meetings and anniversaries organised. Some events were cause for celebration, as in 1992 when the catechetical summer camps for children celebrated their 40th anniversary; others were just plain tragedies, such as the death in a car crash the same year of Dorothy Maria Purchase, President of the Legion of Mary. 1993 was the year of the deacons, with an additional eight permanent deacons ordained, bringing the diocesan total to eleven. Each one was ordained in the parish they were to serve.

1994: Three new canons join the cathedral Chapter (front) Mgr Canon George Hay and Canons Peter Webb and Bartholomew(Bart) Nannery. At back: Canons Bede Davis and David O'Driscoll, Mgr Canon Anthony Gilby and Canons Joseph Richardson and Kevin Rea. Absent were Mgr Canon Michael Hanley and Canon Walter Costello.

The cathedral Chapter had been slightly under strength and so in 1994 three new canons were installed at the cathedral by Bishop Budd – Mgr Canon George Hay of Okehampton, Canon Peter Webb of St Mary's in Poole, and Canon Bart Nannery – bringing the Chapter up to its full complement of Provost (Mgr Anthony Gilby) and nine canons, that is ten in all.

On 26th February 1996 Bishop Restieaux died suddenly at Stoodley Knowle Convent in Torquay, only a day after dining with Bishop Budd and Monsignor Gilby. Bishop Budd remembered him fondly: 'He was our bishop for 31 years and the record of, and the monuments to, his ministry are seen across the diocese. Never once did he try to influence anything I was doing (no matter how mad it was!) and it was always a smiling face that greeted me whenever

RIGHT: Bishop Vaughan, Bishop Graham and Bishop Keily laid to rest beneath the floor of the Lady Chapel with Bishop Restieaux.

122 1858-2008 PLYMOUTH CATHEDRAL

The Decade of Evangelism

THE LAST THIRTY YEARS

I called to see him.' Bishop Restieaux was buried beneath the cathedral's Lady Chapel where, the following December, he was joined by three of his predecessors. For some time the bishop and Chapter had been concerned about the neglected condition of the graves of Bishops Vaughan, Kiely and Graham and so, having negotiated the relevant (and complicated) bureaucracy, their remains were exhumed and came home to the cathedral.

One of Bishop Budd's long-held ambitions came to fruition on 3rd August 1997 with the opening of the first Diocesan Assembly. He had first mooted the idea in 1989 but it was not until 1995 that a co-ordinating group was formed, with Fr Paul Billington as Assembly facilitator and Sister Patricia Short as Assembly administrator. Parish renewal teams were formed and the first year concluded with the publication of the collated feedback in the form of the Assembly booklet, *Towards Our Light*. Exeter University was the venue for the assembly, which got off to a slightly shaky start in August 1997 when David Watt, Chairperson of the Assembly, had to interrupt Evening Prayer to get the delegates to park their cars legally and safely! From then on, however, the week was a great success. Sister Patricia recalled: '…275 delegates had set aside a whole week to explore what it meant to be members of the church in mission here in the South West. The bad weather, the physical hardship of getting from one place to another and the acute shortage of car-parking space did nothing to dampen the spirit of generosity and good will that was evident as we grew in community. We were inspired by gifted

EXETER: The Peter Chalk Centre.

ABOVE: Diocesan Assembly delegates take a break in the coffee lounge.

LEFT: Bishop Christopher celebrated the closing Mass in the University's Great Hall.

INSET: Sister Patricia Short.

THE LAST THIRTY YEARS   *The Decade of Evangelism*

speakers and united in prayer which formed an integral part of the whole proceedings.'

Bishop Budd, reviewing the Assembly, said, 'I hope our parishes will address three things. Firstly, they are all cordially invited into renewed covenant with the poor in order to indicate clearly our commitment into the new millennium to the dignity of every human being. Secondly, I hope all parishes through a process of prayer and reflection will visit again that central question of faith "Who is my neighbour?" Thirdly, I invite all parishes to examine the way they currently live and organise themselves to assess who has access to opportunities for Christian formation.'

> **'We were inspired by gifted speakers and united in prayer.'**
>
> **Sister Patricia Short**

Several stalwarts of the diocese made their exits. Florence (Flo) Pedrick died in January 1995 after a life of service to the diocese; her younger brother Philip survived her and celebrated the Diamond Jubilee of his ordination in 1998. Canon Elwell passed on in 1995 and Canon Kennedy in 1997; and the whole cathedral parish was much shocked by the sudden death of Sister Mary Camillus Rock of the Sisters of St Anne. Exits were balanced by entrances: in 1998, for instance, Frs Michael Kirkpatrick, Philip Dyson, David Williams, Brian Stevens and Dylan James were ordained.

RIGHT: Canon Elwell (top) and Canon Kennedy.

One of the decisions of the Diocesan Assembly had been to set up the Plymouth Diocesan Pastoral Council. It had now come to fruition and on June 12th 1999 the bishop welcomed delegates from around the diocese to the inaugural meeting at Notre Dame School.

The decade of evangelism was drawing to a close and the millennium was just around the corner. A confident, thriving diocese and a freshly re-ordered cathedral were looking forward to its challenges.

The Decade of Evangelism   **THE LAST THIRTY YEARS**

Father Michael Kirkpatrick

I WAS BORN, shortly after the Second World War, and brought up in Glasgow. My grandfather was an 'Elder of the Kirk' and from my earliest years I was taken to Sunday school and to Church. The emphasis in the Presbyterian services and in the RE at school (Glasgow Academy) was entirely on scripture. In my early teens, through a Scout church parade, I came into contact with Anglicanism and was very much drawn by the beauty of liturgical and sacramental worship, which was previously unknown to me, and this led to my Confirmation. From my very first visits to church as a child I was fascinated by the variety of wonderful sounds which came from the pipe organ and I developed a love of music which has remained with me - no that anyone would guess from my attempts at playing the organ!

When I left school it was to follow in the family sea-faring tradition – my father was a Master Mariner and my mother, a WREN during the War, often accompanied him on long voyages – and I came to Plymouth to join the Royal Navy. Although I thoroughly enjoyed life at sea and travelling around the world, I was becoming increasingly aware of a vocation to ministry and, after seven years, I left the Navy for Anglican Theological College. After four years at Durham and Chichester (two of my classmates are also now priests of this diocese) I went back to my native Scotland to be a curate at Elgin in Morayshire and was ordained as an Anglican priest in Inverness Cathedral on St. Patrick's Day 1974. I returned to Plymouth in 1976 to be chaplain at Devonport Hospital and was also in charge of the local parish. I spent three years in North Devon and then was appointed to another Plymouth parish until my decision to resign and seek full Communion with the Catholic Church.

1998: Father Michael Kirkpatrick, a former Anglican clergyman, gives his first blessing after his ordination.

I attended the special course for former Anglican clergy organised by Cardinal Hume at Archbishop's House and Allen Hall Seminary, Westminster. I also embarked upon a five year course leading to a Pontifical degree at Maryvale Institute, Birmingham and am now in the final year. Since my resignation I have been working in the Cathedral Parish where I have been made very welcome. I am kept busy between parish and the bishop's office but I still manage to find time for daily walks with 'Tiber', my Greyhound-Lurcher.

Father Michael Kirkpatrick. *Cathedral Parish and Bishop's Secretary.*

THE LAST THIRTY YEARS *The Decade of Evangelism*

The bright and beautiful interior of Plymouth Cathedral, ready for the challenges and opportunities of a new millennium.

A new century **THE LAST THIRTY YEARS**

Chapter Twelve

THE DAWN OF the millennium was something of a disappointment for the prophets of doom: planes didn't fall out of the sky; the global financial systems remained steady without a trace of meltdown; and there was no apocalypse.

In his foreword to the 2000 Year Book, Bishop Christopher wrote of the importance of the millennium: 'We are entering a very special year: the year of the Jubilee of the Incarnation of Our Lord Jesus Christ. I would like to encourage you all to wear proudly your Catholic/Christian credentials and to bring to bear on the issues of the day some insight into what it means to be human, because 'the Word was made flesh and dwelt among us.' To this end, the Word, in the form of the Book of Gospels, was enthroned on the high altar for the duration.

2000: The whole world celebrated the Millennium.

For the Diocese of Plymouth, the year was cause for a double celebration, as it marked the 150th anniversary of its formation. On January 1st, Bishop Christopher re-affirmed the dedication of the diocese to Our Lady, the first event in a series which was to celebrate the dual anniversary. Later the same month the cathedral was the venue for the ecumenical 'Spirit of the Millennium' exhibition during Christian Unity Week, and hosted Plymouth's annual service which was attended by all the city's Church leaders and the Lord Mayor.

As ever, away from the 'headline' events, the business of cathedral and diocese continued. People from all over the diocese packed the cathedral in March for the RCIA Rite of Election and just before

LEFT: The 150th anniversary seal of the Catholic Bishops' Conference of England and Wales.

PLYMOUTH CATHEDRAL 1858-2008   127

THE LAST THIRTY YEARS *A new century*

RIGHT:
The Diocese of Plymouth celebrated the 150th anniversary of its formation.

BELOW:
Two of the embroidered silk banners by Nina Humphreys next to the Ambo.

Easter a similarly large contingent of priests from Devon, Cornwall and Dorset attended the Chrism Mass to collect the Holy Oils and take them back to their parishes. On Good Friday an open air Stations of the Cross, in conjunction with St Peter's Anglican Church and Wesley Methodist, expressed a public witness of faith and allowed the priests and laity to renew their joint 'Covenant with the Poor.' The RCIA Thanksgiving Mass was followed by the Annual Naval Mass, held for the first time in the cathedral.

On 23rd September the voices of the cathedral bell and a lone trumpet called the people to prayer to celebrate the diocese's 150th birthday. The Anglican bishops of Truro and Plymouth and other church leaders were welcomed at the cathedral door by Bishop Christopher and Canon Nannery – an act of hospitality that, as the bishop remarked, would have been unthinkable 150, 100 or even 50 years ago. The Lord Mayor and his wife attended, as did Lord and Lady Clifford, representing the old Catholic families who had sustained the faith through difficult times over the centuries. Banners representing every deanery and proclaiming the Diocesan Vision Statement were carried in and Mass celebrated by a large congregation which included Archbishop Bowen, Metropolitan bishop of the Southwark Province, and several other bishops. A huge marquee had been set up in the cathedral car park and over 700 guests were able to enjoy good food and drink and a birthday cake.

To mark the new millennium, Nina Humphreys, a Cornish teacher of design and embroidery, was commissioned to produce new hangings around the Ambo. The images, of the four evangelists as angels, were inspired by the Book of Revelations and the prophecies of Ezechiel, where there are descriptions of winged figures with the

A *new century*

THE LAST THIRTY YEARS

appearance of a Man, a Lion, a Calf and an Eagle.

The diocesan awards ceremony in October saw awards presented to three cathedral parishioners: Frank Tregaskis, Mary Metherell and Frank Payne who, at 96, was the cathedral's oldest parishioner. The retirement of Fr John Bolland – National Clergy Golfer of the year in 1993, by the way – had led to his parish of Holy Cross being paired with the cathedral, and in December Holy Cross, along with the cathedral and St Joseph's in Devonport, held a Christmas party at the Royal Fleet Club, putting the seal on a memorable year.

CLERGY GOLFER OF THE YEAR

Clergy Champion Golfer – Father John Bolland.

Father John Bolland, parish priest of Holy Cross, Beaumont Road.

Church Unity was in the limelight in 2001 when hundreds gathered at Exeter Cathedral to renew their commitment and celebrate the tenth anniversary of the original ecumenical covenants. These committed the leaders of all denominations to encourage fuller understanding and closer co-operation between the churches of Devon. Bishop Christopher, a signatory of the original covenant, attended and recalled how the initiative had led to a regular Church Leaders' meeting and genuine friendship. Later that year, the bishop was honoured by Newman College in Birmingham with an Honorary Life Fellowship in recognition of his work there between 1971 and 1976 as a Lecturer of Theology and Head of Department.

2001: Bishop Christopher receives an Honorary Life Fellowship from Newman College in Birmingham.

PLYMOUTH CATHEDRAL 1858-2008

THE LAST THIRTY YEARS   *A new century*

The 207 ft spire of the cathedral was in need of substantial repairs and a Tower Fund was launched in spring 2002 to raise the £250,000 necessary for the work, which was to be overseen by diocesan surveyor Bob Whitemore and architect Simon Crosbie.

June and July 2002 were busy months. Bishop Christopher celebrated his Ruby (40th) Jubilee on 8th July at a diocesan Mass, at which Canon Nannery gave the homily and said: 'One or two priests occasionally ask what it's like in such close proximity to the bishop? Not bad really; he is extremely quiet, he hardly ever makes a sound coming in or going out or getting up at six in the morning, for which I am most grateful ... Bishop Christopher has, however, a lovely and subtle way of getting his messages across when he wants to, without making a fuss or creating a scene ... On one occasion the second collection for Racial Justice Sunday at the cathedral had been omitted, something which clearly hadn't escaped his notice. Instead of commenting about the cathedral dean's lack of concern for the racially ill-treated, he came over from Bishop's House and gave the counters his contribution for the collection which had never taken place. One has to admit it was a master stroke in getting the point across. Message received!'

2004: Work in progress on the cathedral's spire.

Another anniversary was the centenary of Our Most Holy Redeemer Church in Keyham, celebrated on 6th July with a flower festival and centenary Mass, while Fr Bernard Hahesy celebrated his golden jubilee and Frs Michael Lock and Ted Buckley their silver.

A new century THE LAST THIRTY YEARS

1852-2002: Canons' celebration. Standing (l-r) Canons Bernard Jaffa, Chris Smith, Peter Webb, Patrick Costello, Bede Davis and Joseph Richardson. Seated: Mgr George Hay (Provost), Canon Bart Nannery, Archbishop Pablo Puente, Mgr Anthony Gilby, Bishop Christopher Budd and Canon Henry Doyle. Missing: Mgr Robert Draper, VG.

The 'big event' of 2002 was the visit of the Papal Nuncio, His Excellency Archbishop Pablo Puente, which took place from 28th June to 2nd July, and coincided with the 150th anniversary of the Chapter of Plymouth Cathedral. After lunch with the Chapter, the archbishop preached at evening prayer and then attended a reception in his honour in a marquee in the cathedral garden. The next four days were a whirlwind of visits and meetings. There was Mass at Buckfast Abbey, a prayer meeting for peace at Launceston Town Hall, a reception for the Cornwall Deanery at Lanivet, and a visit to Exeter, where the archbishop saw St Nicholas School, Rosary House, the Guildhall and presided at Mass at Sacred Heart Church. The final day of the visit was spent in

LEFT: Bishop Christopher with the Apostolic Nuncio, Archbishop Pablo Puente.

THE LAST THIRTY YEARS — A new century

the Dorset Deanery, with a visit to St Edward's school in Poole and Mass at St Mary's.

On 27th October Fr John Kinane died in Ireland. A much-loved parish priest who had served at the cathedral, Yelverton, Weymouth, Plymstock (where he completed the church), Beacon Park, Keyham and Poole.

Another passing was that of Canon Philip Pedrick in January 2003. A true son of the cathedral parish, he was born, brought up and lived the last seventeen years of his life in the same house just a hundred yards from the cathedral. He worked at many parishes and his contribution is best summed up in the words of Canon Nannery: 'Phil never spared himself in the service of the Lord. He was the most dedicated and committed priest one is ever likely to meet. He possessed an innocence and simplicity, coupled with a wisdom and an ability to accept graciously whatever life threw at him.'

Canon Pedrick had been a dear friend of Barbara Tyacke, the cook and housekeeper at Cathedral House, and who died on 6th March 2003. Shortly before her death at Nazareth House, she told Canon Nannery: '...everybody here is very kind; but what I want now is for the Lord to take me home in heaven.' On being told of Canon Pedrick's death, her reply was simple: 'I hope he gets me a place up there quickly.'

A few months later, Canon Nannery was speaking at the funeral Mass of Sister Raphael who had spent the last eight years of her life at the cathedral. She was a Daughter of the Cross from Stoodley Knowle Convent in Torquay and together with her life-long friend Sister Dolores

ABOVE: Canon Philip Pedrick enjoying his retirement in the bishop's garden and, inset, as a young priest.

RIGHT: Barbara Tyacke.

1858-2008 PLYMOUTH CATHEDRAL

A new century **THE LAST THIRTY YEARS**

2003: Bishop Christopher greets the Holy Father during his Ad Limina visit.

and two other sisters looked after the Exposition of the Blessed Sacrament and the sacristy. "Sister served the people of the cathedral parish with a loyal love and a pure heart," he said.

Pope John Paul II celebrated his silver jubilee in 2003 and in the same year Bishop Christopher made his five-yearly *Ad Limina* visit to Rome, where, on 16th October, he concelebrated the Holy Father's jubilee Mass. The bishop's departure was bittersweet: 'I felt sadness as I went to the airport. I suspect I have spoken to and seen Pope John Paul for the last time. He was the pope who appointed me as bishop and who has been pope during the whole of the eighteen years here in Plymouth. It is most important that we keep him in our prayers during the coming months.'

Work on the spire was completed in 2004. There was new stonework, repointing and weatherproofing; woodwork and metalwork was replaced and a new steel spiral staircase and lighting installed. Of the final bill of £275,000, nearly £200,000 was covered by grants from English Heritage and the Places of Worship Grant Scheme, while the remaining £75,000 was raised by the parish. The first 130ft was done from scaffolding and the highest work was done by a mason slung in a bosun's chair over 200ft up! Richard Parker, of Exeter

Work on the spire was completed in 2004. The highest work was done by a mason slung in a bosun's chair over 200 feet up!

PLYMOUTH CATHEDRAL 1858-2008

THE LAST THIRTY YEARS   *A new century*

The Saint Boniface window at the west end of the cathedral shows scenes from the life of our patron saint.

1858-2008 PLYMOUTH CATHEDRAL

A new century

THE LAST THIRTY YEARS

Archaeology, recognised the spire's importance: 'The spire remains a landmark building, and a fine example of continental (particularly French) architecture on Victorian Gothic during the mid 19th Century.'

2004 was also the 1250th anniversary of the martyrdom of the diocesan patron Saint Boniface, an occasion which was celebrated not only in the diocese but all over Europe. At Crediton, St Boniface's birthplace, the bishop and local priests concelebrated Mass on June 5th, the saint's feast day. A week later in Dokkum, Holland, where St Boniface was martyred, Cardinal Simmonis, Archbishop of Utrecht, concelebrated Mass with many other priests, including Canon Nannery who represented the Plymouth Diocese. Finally, the martyrdom was celebrated in the cathedral on 30th June.

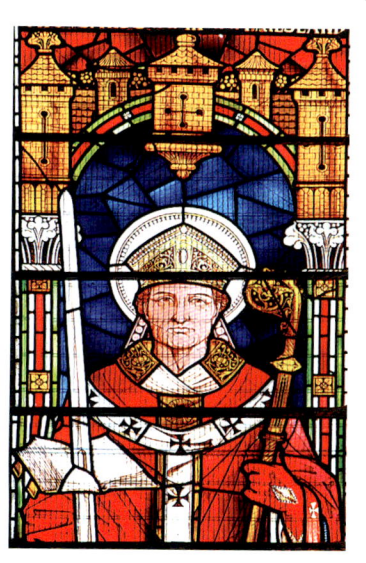

LEFT: Detail from the Saint Boniface window.

BELOW Saint Julie Billiart, who founded the Sisters of Notre Dame.

The Sisters of Notre Dame de Namur celebrated the 200th anniversary of the founding of their Order; celebrations had been building up over the past two years, with an opening ceremony at Christ the King in May 2002, a week of meditation and talks in Truro the following October, and a tea party at Notre Dame House in 2003. As an adjunct to the celebrations, Notre Dame School held a grand reunion at which (appropriately) 200 guests from as far back as the nineteen-thirties were able to share memories of their time at the school. For the older alumni, the school was unrecognisable and change was ongoing – plans were soon to be announced for a £4 million programme to provide a new four-court sports hall and fitness suite, with the hope that this would be a precursor to a rebuild of the whole school.

The 2006 Year Book was the fiftieth in the series.

THE LAST THIRTY YEARS

A new century

For years it had been edited by Father (now Canon) Chris Smith and the 2006 issue was to be his last. In it, he reflected on what had undoubtedly been the most important piece of news in the Catholic world for many years: 'We might say that the death of the pope took place in the full light of publicity as the world watched a very ill man with Parkinson's disease slowly and patiently preparing for God's final call, while still continuing his work as much as he was able. But what took us completely by surprise was the universal interest it aroused among so many of all races, colours and creeds. The media interest was to be overwhelming with blanket TV and press coverage all over the world.' The Conclave elected as his successor Cardinal Joseph Ratzinger, who took the name Benedict XVI.

There were other departures that barely registered outside the diocese, but were no less important in their way. Canon Walter Costello, who had been a priest in the diocese for nearly 70 years, died in November 2004. He was one of the few who could still remember the bombing of the cathedral, and had founded the Plymouth Group 179 of the Handicapped Children's Pilgrimage Trust (HCPT). Canon Bede Davis died in June 2006; he had served in several parishes and been cathedral administrator.

The new pope, Benedict XVI. (L'Osservatore Romano)

The deaths of these two men, who had given so much of themselves for the diocese and cathedral over many decades, was a reminder of the sense of continuity that the story of the cathedral represents, a continuity celebrated in the 150th anniversary events of 2008.

There is the continuity represented in stones and mortar, exemplified by that elegant spire pointing to the heavens; and the continuity of all the people who have contributed to the story. There is Bishop Vaughan and his great vision; Herbert Woodman manning his ARP post in the blitz; there are parishioners, housekeepers, sisters and even Molly the cat. All have had their roles to play and all are part of the whole story of a people that is Plymouth's proud cathedral – a spiritual beacon that shines its light forward into the twenty-first century.

All have had their roles to play and all are part of the whole story of a people.

Sister Mary Peter Scully, SSA

SISTER PETER died on 14th October 2006 aged 94 years and in her 70th year as a professed religious. She became a Sister of St Anne just before World War Two and was arguably the life and soul of the cathedral parish. Just ten years earlier she celebrated the 60th anniversary of her profession. At a special Mass of thanksgiving at Plymouth Cathedral, she received a Papal Blessing and afterwards joined family, friends and parishioners for a celebration party and buffet. In her inimitable style she entertained us with a few Irish airs and jigs on her violin. He violin and accordion are well-used and well-travelled. They have helped her to bring joy, hope and fun into the lives of many; some of whom were in desperate straits.

"I started my work in the East End of London. Our convent in Rotherhythe was in a area of grinding poverty," she said. "We were often out with soup kitchens feeding the poor,' she said. "There were long lines of poor men. It was this work among the most deprived of God's people which strengthened my vocation and gave it impetus."

She actually started as a postulant and novice in January 1936. "It was the Legion of Mary – then quite a new organisation – which inspired my vocation when I was a young woman," she explained. She had spent seven years as a member of the Legion at Cork Cathedral near her home in Ireland.

She arrived in Plymouth in time for the Blitz. She worked here throughout the war in catechesis and parish work. The sisters helped bombed out families and comforted the bereaved. Their nursing skills were in constant demand. But shortly after the war, she was asked to work in a remote hospital in the northern region of Ghana, West Africa. "I went originally just to do the books!" Her bookkeeping and secretarial skills had been acquired at Skerry's College in Cork.

With Sister Raphael and Sister John she went out to Africa to an empty and abandoned hospital. There was no priest, no church and no school. "We went to help the White Fathers start their mission in Gonja after the war, " said Sister Peter. The medical skills of the Sisters of St. Anne were employed to get the hospital and mobile clinic going. Soon Sister Peter was drafted into the dispensary to help the doctor and that was the start of her career in pharmacy.

She returned to London for three years to study pharmacy and chemistry and to gain practical dispensing experience at Guy's Hospital. Once fully qualified in compounding and dispensing medicines she returned to Ghana to take charge of the hospital's pharmacy and stayed for a very happy 14 years. In 1978 she returned to work in Plymouth Cathedral parish.

Reviewing her career and ministry, her feelings are best expressed by her favourite quotation from Tennyson's 'Morte d'Arthur': 'I have lived my life, and that which I have done, may He within Himself make pure ... more things are wrought by prayer than this world dreams of.'

THE LAST THIRTY YEARS *A new century*

The Chapel of Reconciliation. A private room at the west end of the cathedral where confessions may be heard.

Appendix
PART V ~ *Appendix.*

Contents

CHOLERA IN PLYMOUTH (1850)	... ...	140
THE FIRST VATICAN COUNCIL	... ...	140
MEMORIAL WINDOWS	... ...	141
STATIONS OF THE CROSS	... ...	143
THE IMPACT OF VATICAN II	... ...	145
CHRONOLOGY OF DATES	... ...	146
THE BISHOPS OF THE DIOCESE	... ...	151
ADMINISTRATORS AND DEANS	... ...	151
OUR PRIMARY SCHOOLS	... ...	151
PICTURE CREDITS	... ...	151
MEET THE AUTHOR	... ...	151
MAIN INDEX	... ...	152

The cathedral's Paschal candle, with detail, left.

Cholera in Plymouth

THE STATE of sanitation in the middle of the nineteenth century was almost incredibly bad. Successive spasms of mushroom building, almost unplanned, accompanied the mushroom growth of population; but the building rushes did not supply a quarter of the need. A desperate congestion resulted.

The first epidemic struck down 1,884 people of whom 779 died.

When Government inspectors were called in to report on two outbreaks of cholera in 1832 and 1849, the picture beggared their descriptive powers. The first epidemic struck down 1,884 people, of whom 779 died. The second was even more disastrous, with 3,360 people infected and 1,894 dead. This gave a death rate from cholera alone in 1849 of about 4 per cent of the inhabitants. That is not surprising when we note that between 1840 and 1850 the population increased by over 13,000, but the number of dwellings by only 900. Owners divided and subdivided houses till it became the exception to find only one family in one house, however small. A high proportion of the buildings dated from centuries back. They stood in narrow streets or lanes or courtyards. Waterborne drainage was rare; one room to a family, if not a rule, was a common phenomenon. Plymouth's stood seventh on the list of cholera death rates in English towns.

From 'The Story of Plymouth' by R. A. J. Walling (1950).

The First Vatican Council

BISHOP VAUGHAN did not write a pastoral letter for Advent 1869, Canon Woollett did, as the bishop was away in Rome attending the First Vatican Council, *writes Tom Healy*. The event was brought to a hasty end by the Franco-Prussian War and the occupation of Rome by soldiers of the United Italy.

Bishop Vaughan does not seem to have been very enthusiastic about the Declaration of Papal Infallibility; he was not alone in this. Archbishop Mc Hale of Tuam in the West of Ireland was none too keen either, but he realised that it was God's way of working to strengthen the authority of the Church and he supported it.

After all in one of his early pastorals he criticised the Church of England for its doctrinal laxity so he could hardly have taken a casual stance towards infallibility.

Appendix

Memorial windows

MISS ANN LETITIA Trelawney of Trelawne was the daughter of the famous Sir Harry Trelawney (1756-1834) and was one of the original benefactors of the cathedral. She gave Bishop Vaughan a gift of £3,000 towards the building costs.

The Blessed Sacrament chapel in the south transept is surrounded by an iron screen, also a gift of Miss Trelawney, and she donated £27 for the stained glass (right) in the chapel which depicts St Henry and St Ann, her father's patron saint and her own.

After the death of his wife in 1821, the Rev Sir Harry Trelawney, below, became a Catholic priest and in 1830

PLYMOUTH CATHEDRAL — *Appendix*

was ordained in Rome by Cardinal Carlo Odescalchi (1786-1841) when nearly 74. He had inherited the baronetcy and family estate at Trelawne near Polperro in 1772 at the age of 16, and was a descendant of Bishop Trelawny whose trial in the 17th century gave rise to the chorus: 'And shall Trelawny live? Or shall Trelawny die? Here's twenty thousand Cornishmen, Shall know the reason why.'

He became one of the greatest landowners in the neighbourhood of Polperro, with hundreds of acres of land to the west of Looe as well as elsewhere in Cornwall.

Sir Harry was an unusual character who became, in turn, a Methodist minister, an Anglican vicar and eventually a Catholic priest. His hospitality to a Catholic priest who had fled the French Revolution led to his daughters founding Sclerder Abbey nearby.

The Rev Sir Harry Trelawny was head of one of Cornwall's foremost families and a magistrate. He contributed to the repair of Polperro harbour following a terrifying storm there in 1817.

After his ordination, he remained in Italy until his death in 1834 at Laveno, where he is buried.

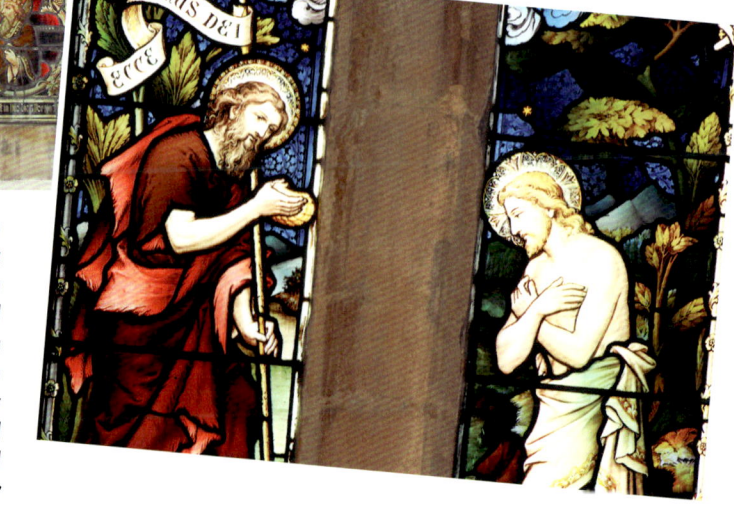

This window in the south-west corner of the cathedral (detail, right) is a memorial to Winifred Mary Pike who died on 3rd November 1903.

Appendix PLYMOUTH CATHEDRAL

The Chapter of Canons in 1906. Standing: Canons Daniel Kennedy, Joseph Higgins, Walter Keily, Bernard Wade, Charles Langdon. Seated: Leo Croutelle, George Poole (Provost), His Lordship Bishop Charles Graham, Thomas Courtenay and John Keily. (see chapter three)

The Stations of the Cross

THE ORIGINAL Stations of the Cross were erected in 1894 and blessed by the Bishop of Clifton who, as Monsignor Brownlow, had formerly been the Provost of the cathedral Chapter and Vicar General of the Plymouth Diocese.

The Stations which you see at present were carved in 1958 by Joseph Cribb of Ditchling from stone which came from the quarries at Beer on the south Devon coast.

These are the quarries in the south-east corner of Devon which, centuries ago, provided the stone for the building of Exeter Cathedral.

One of the original Stations of the Cross is seen in this photo of Canon Cantell pointing at post war damage.

Some of the Stations of the Cross of Plymouth Cathedral.

The impact of Vatican II

THE SECOND VATICAN COUNCIL convened in the autumn of 1962 and continued, at intervals, for the next several years. To those of us who lived through it its changes came in great swathes.

By Advent 1964, English had replaced Latin in the celebration of Mass, a shock to many older Catholics who had been brought up to believe that this common dead language was the bedrock of the liturgy. To others it brought the Mass closer to them and enabled them to relate more intimately to the great mysteries of the sacrament.

The change by which the congregation faced the priest or rather the priest now faced the congregation also created some upheaval in the minds of many of the devout. Change was happening and often at a pace which overwhelmed not only the people but also many of their clergy. The changes in the reception of Holy Communion which had been begun as far back as the pontificate of Pope Pius X and, continued by Pius XII now gathered speed. Receiving Holy Communion in the hand, receiving it under both kinds all created mighty upheavals of mind, spirit and, in churches, of logistics and architecture.

The task of preparing the cathedral to implement these alterations fell to the administrator, Canon Joseph Elwell. As the bishop's agent it was his responsibility, along with his fellow canons and clergy, to put ideas into form. It was in many ways a daunting task, not least because it involved leading both clergy and people to understand what was being created and to accept it. This was probably the greatest set of alterations to the practice of the faith since the Council of Trent responded to the Protestant Reformation of the 16th century, and, like Trent it did not always go down well or easily.

A first requirement was to brief the clergy of the diocese and, through them, the numerous congregations. This took time and involved a great deal of preparation. The post Vatican Two liturgy may now be second nature to us but it was not so to begin with and it is down to the work of clergy like Canon Elwell that these changes were explained, put into practice and, in time, accepted by the overwhelming mass of the people.

Changing the position of the altar, especially in a church like the cathedral, was a formidable task and involved both muscle and brain for anything ill-prepared might have damaged or destroyed a priceless piece of work. Yet it was done and in a way which, looking back at it from the vantage point of forty years, seems quite imperceptible.

Tom Healy

PLYMOUTH CATHEDRAL   *Appendix*

Chronology

...a selection of principal dates, mainly from the text.

1829 Catholic Emancipation Act resulted in a more relaxed public attitude towards Catholicism.
1840 England divided into eight Vicariates by Pope Gregory XVI.
1848 The Great Western Railway came to Plymouth.
1850 Apostolic letter *Universalis Ecclesiae* of Pope Pius IX restored the Hierarchy of England and Wales with a metropolitan see at Westminster and twelve suffragan sees including Plymouth.
1851 Ecclesiastical Titles Act prohibited Catholic hierarchy from adopting existing ecclesiastical titles, accompanied by anti-Catholic agitation.
1851 Dr George Errington consecrated first Bishop of Plymouth by Cardinal Wiseman on 25th July.
1852 The Cathedral Chapter of Canons 'erected' on 6th April. Bishop Errington opened a school in Granby Street, which later moved to Chapel Street, Devonport.
1853 The Plymouth Cathedral Chapter inaugurated by Bishop Errington.
1854 First Diocesan Synod at Ugbrooke Park.
1854 Proclamation of the dogma of the Immaculate Conception of the Blessed Virgin Mary by Pope Pius IX.
1855 Bishop Errington created Archbishop. Moves to London to be Cardinal Wiseman's co-adjutor.
1855 William Vaughan, the cathedral's founder, consecrated second Bishop of Plymouth on 16th September by Cardinal Wiseman.
1856 Bishop Vaughan purchases 'Five Fields', the site of Plymouth Cathedral on 20th February. Bishop Vaughan founded St Boniface's college in Plymouth's Wyndham Square.
1857 Collapse of cathedral roof during construction due to gunnery practice in Plymouth Sound.

1858 Plymouth's Roman Catholic Cathedral of St Mary and St Boniface opened for worship on the Feast of the Annunciation; 25th March. 'I am the Immaculate Conception' – Our Lady appears to [Saint] Bernadette Soubirous at Lourdes for the ninth time ... on 25th March. Canon Herbert Woollett becomes the cathedral's first administrator.
1859 A pulpit of Caen stone erected in the cathedral.
1860 Six Sisters of Notre Dame de Namur arrived in Plymouth at the invitation of Bishop Vaughan.
1861 Secular Clergy Fund founded by Canon Woollett. Church of St Michael and St Joseph opened in Devonport.
1864 A stone altar, designed by John Hanson, fixed in the Blessed Sacrament chapel. Foundation stone laid for the new Convent of Notre Dame in Wyndham Street, next to the cathedral.
1867 Spire added to Plymouth Cathedral.
1869 - 70 First Vatican Council.
1874 Plymouth's new Guildhall opened on August 13th.
1875 Canon Patrick Sheehan starts his two year curacy at the cathedral.
1876 Gas lighting installed in the cathedral.
1880 Episcopal silver jubilee of Bishop Vaughan. West window of St Boniface installed. Consecration of cathedral, now free of debt.
1881 Original (1854) foundation stone of Holy Cross, Beaumont Road, blessed on 15th April after the whole church was re-erected, having been moved from Teignmouth due to railway works.
1884 Benedictine monks of Pierre-qui-vire purchase the site of Buckfast Abbey.
1885 Cathedral struck by lightning. Spire re-pointed during repairs.
1886 Death of Archbishop Errington, founder of the Diocese of Plymouth.
1888 Death of Canon Woollett, the cathedral's first administrator.
1889 30-foot high reredos installed behind

Appendix

the high altar.

1892 Canon Charles Graham elected co-adjutor for Bishop Vaughan and ordained titular Bishop of Cisamus on 28th October with right of succession. Bishop Vaughan retired.

1893 Monsignor Brownlow appointed to the vacant Provostship of the Cathedral Chapter,

1895 Bishop Vaughan hosts the Fifth Diocesan Synod at the cathedral.

1897 Rev John Keily, Diocesan Inspector of Schools created a canon of the Cathedral Chapter.

1898 Plymouth Cathedral spire again hit by lightning, damaging the new electric clock.

1902 Death of Bishop William Vaughan on 25th October. Bishop Graham succeeds to the title as the third Bishop of Plymouth.

1911 Death of Bishop Graham on 2nd September. Canon John Keily consecrated fourth Bishop of Plymouth by Cardinal Bourne.

1912 The Third Home Rule Bill approved by Parliament for Ireland.

1913 Fourth National Catholic Congress held in Plymouth.

1914 City of Plymouth formed in October by the amalgamation of the three towns of Devonport, Stonehouse and Plymouth (Sutton).

1914 - 18 First World War.

1916 Easter Rising in Dublin. Irish Presentation Brothers at St Boniface's College.

1919 Cardinal Bourne consecrated the new Carmelite monastery at Efford.

1920 Partition introduced to Ireland. (1921: Irish Free State Treaty).

1921 Inauguration of Launceston Pilgrimage in honour of the martyred Blessed Cuthbert Mayne (canonised in 1970).

1922 Election of Pope Pius XI.

1923 Canon Mahoney appointed cathedral administrator.

1926 Catholic Relief [Emancipation] Act repealed most of the remaining legal disabilities of Catholics. General Strike.

PLYMOUTH CATHEDRAL

1927 Bishop Keily created Bishop Assistant at the Pontifical Throne by Pope Pius XI and celebrated his golden jubilee.

1928 Death of Bishop Keily on 23rd Sept.

1929 Bishop John Barrett transferred to Plymouth from Birmingham on 7th June and became the fifth Bishop of Plymouth.

1930 Golden jubilee of the consecration of the cathedral on 22nd September.

1931 St Boniface's College move to Beaconfield, to be run by the Irish Christian Brothers. Poor Sisters of Nazareth arrive from Exeter to run orphanage at Hartley. Canon Jeremiah Ryan becomes cathedral administrator.

1932 Sisters of St Anne, founded in 1911, invited to form a community in Wyndham Square by Bishop Barrett. Consecration of Buckfast Abbey.

1933 Poor Sisters of Nazareth move orphanage to Nazareth House on the site of the Earl of Mount Edgecumbe's waterside Winter Villa in Durnford Street, Stonehouse.

1939 Death of Pope Pius XI.

1939 Blessing of Dom Bruno Fehrenbacher, Abbot of Buckfast, by Bishop Barrett.

1939 - 45 Second World War.

1940 Canon Jeremiah Ryan, cathedral administrator, successfully terminates a riot by IRA prisoners at Dartmoor Prison. First civilian casualties of German bombs in Stonehouse.

1941 Intense air raids. Blitz of Plymouth by hundreds of Luftwaffe planes. St Boniface's pupils evacuated to Buckfast and Notre Dame schoolgirls to Teignmouth.

1946 Death of Bishop Barrett on 2nd November.

1947 Consecration of Bishop Francis Grimshaw as sixth Bishop of Plymouth on 25th July at the cathedral by Archbishop Masterson of Birmingham.

1948 Rt Hon Sir Francis Lesser PC, former MP and Lord Justice of Appeal received into the Catholic Church at Yelverton and confirmed by Bishop Grimshaw.

1950 Centenary of the Restoration of the

PLYMOUTH CATHEDRAL *Appendix*

Catholic Hierarchy of England and Wales celebrated with a Pontifical High Mass at the cathedral sung by Archbishop Masterson with a homily by Bishop Grimshaw.

1951 Canon George Cantell becomes cathedral administrator.

1952 'Peter' the new cathedral bell fixed in the spire. This was the gift of Father John Haslip in memory of his mother.

1953 Cardinal Bernard Griffin visits Plymouth to celebrate the 100th anniversary of the Plymouth Cathedral Chapter. He donated £3,000 towards the restoration of the cathedral.

1954 Bishop Grimshaw appeals for more funds to restore the cathedral and repair bomb damage. The Catenian Association donated £1,000. Bishop Grimshaw appointed Archbishop of Birmingham after death of Archbishop Masterson.

1954 1200th anniversary of the death of St Boniface. Pontifical High Mass at Buckfast Abbey celebrated by Cardinal Frings, Archbishop of Cologne. 12,000 at Plymouth Argyle's football ground at Home Park for pageant and celebrations.

1955 Monsignor Cyril Restieaux consecrated seventh Bishop of Plymouth at the cathedral by Archbishop Grimshaw, his predecessor, on 14th June.

1957 Carmelite convent at Efford closed and becomes Parish of Efford with Fr Ian Jones as first parish priest. First Diocesan Year Book publishe by Canon O'Malley.

1958 Brother Edward Quinn, retired teacher at St Boniface's, received an Apostolic Blessing from the Holy Father, presented by Bishop Restieaux, to celebrate his diamond jubilee as a Christian Brother.

1958 Solemn High Mass at the cathedral sung by Canon Cantell on 25th March to celebrate the centenary of the opening of the cathedral. Official Pontifical High Mass (delayed by Easter) on 1st May sung by Bishop Restieaux with a sermon by Archbishop Grimshaw. Followed by a Mission by two Redemptorist priests.

1961 Bishop Restieaux laid the foundation stone of the church of Christ the King in Armada Way. One of the last commissions of the renowned architect, Sir Giles Gilbert Scott, it was the 'gift of an anonymous lady' later revealed to be Mrs Clare Rye. The church was consecrated in 1962.

1962 - 65 Second Vatican Council.

1965 Province of Southwark established with three suffragan sees including Plymouth. Canon Joseph Elwell appointed as cathedral administrator.

1966 Bishop Restieaux opened the Bishop Vaughan Secondary School at Manadon on 16th March. It was immediately the largest Catholic school in the diocese. He also opened the new buildings at Notre Dame School on 26th September.

1969 The Knights of St Columba (KSC) celebrated their golden jubilee. Plymouth KSC Province pilgrimage to Rome led by Fr Bede Davis. Golden jubilee of Canon Joseph O'Byrne, parish priest of Holy Cross, Beaumont Road.

1969 Opening of the new diocesan shrine to St Boniface at his birthplace in Crediton. Bishop Restieaux laid the foundation stone on 2nd August.

1970 Canonisation of the Forty Martyrs of England and Wales by Pope Paul VI, included St Cuthbert Mayne, a patron of the cathedral. Cardinal Heenan was guest of honour at St Boniface's College speech day on 9th December.

1970 Death of Jack Pedrick after many years of serving Mass at the cathedral and leading the Bishop's Own 14th Plymouth Scout Group. Death of Mgr Jeremiah Ryan, secretary to Bishop Barrett, hero of the blitz and the Dartmoor Prison riot.

1971 Bishop Restieaux opened the new extension to the children's home at Nazareth House in Stonehouse. Britain's coinage decimalised.

1972 Cathedral sanctuary reconstructed to conform to post-Vatican II and liturgical requirements. Death of Canon O'Byrne, parish priest of Holy Chross, Beaumont Road, for over 30 years.

1974 Fred Johnson becomes the first Catholic Lord Mayor of Plymouth since the Reformation. Maurice Heron, an altar

Appendix

server at the cathedral since 1927 and Master of Ceremonies, receives the *Bene Merenti* medal.

1976 First cathedral guide book published in colour. 'Mission to Plymouth', involving all Christian denominations and schools, culminates in an ecumenical rally at Home Park on 4th April.

1977 Silver jubilee of HM The Queen. Fourth centenary of the martyrdom of St Cuthbert Mayne. 6,000 attend annual pilgrimage to Launceston including Cardinal Basil Hume, making his first visit to the diocese.

1977 Golden jubilee of the Sisters of St Anne.

1978 Death of Pope Paul VI on 6th August. His successor, Pope John Paul reigned for only thirty-three days before his death and was succeeded by Pope John Paul II.

1978 Death of Mrs Clare Rye, benefactor of the diocese. In 1951 she had bought the Anglican church in Tavistock in memory of her husband and in 1961 paid anonymously for the building of Christ the King, Armada Way. A stalwart of the Christ the King bookshop, Mrs Alicia O'Leary, received the *Bene Merenti* medal for her long service.

1978 Establishment of the Diocesan Youth Commission with Fr Sean Flannery as youth officer. 800 young people attend Youth Rally at St Rita's, Honiton.

1980 Bishop Restieaux's silver jubilee on 9th April with a concelebrated Mass attended by 70 clerics as well as the Archbishop of Southwark, four other bishops and Cardinal Basil Hume. National Pastoral Congress held in Liverpool.

1980 4,000 Catholics at Mass in Exeter Cathedral to celebrate the 13th centenary of the birth of St Boniface, patron of Plymouth Cathedral. Centenary of the consecration of Plymouth Cathedral on 22nd September. Anniversary Mass broadcast on TV.

1980 Canon Bede Davis appointed administrator of the cathedral. Sister Josephine of the Sisters of St Anne celebrated her golden jubilee.

1981 Centenary of the re-consecration of

PLYMOUTH CATHEDRAL

Holy Cross church in Beaumont Road. St Boniface's College moved to Crownhill and merged with the Bishop Vaughan Secondary School to become a boys' comprehensive. Notre Dame School became a girls' comprehensive.

1982 Visit of Pope John Paul II to Britain. Falklands War. Golden jubilee of the arrival of the Sisters of St Anne in the cathedral parish. Centenary of the consecration of Buckfast Abbey with a Mass of Thanksgiving at which Cardinal Hume presided. Golden jubilee of the ordination of Bishop Restieaux.

1983 First issues of *The Link*, the Plymouth Deanery quarterly magazine. Beaconfield demolished to make way for St Boniface's Park, a housing estate.

1985 St Joseph's new church in Devonport opened and consecrated by Bishop Restieaux in November who retired at the end of the year with a farewell Mass for the clergy on 17th December.

1986 Farewell Mass for the people celebrated by Bishop Restieaux on 11th January.

1986 Enthronement and consecration of Bishop Christopher Budd as the eighth Bishop of Plymouth on 15th January. 700 attended of which there were 160 priests and 21 bishops.

1987 Canon Elwell celebrated the golden jubilee of his priesthood.

1987 Brother Sreenan retired as headmaster of St Boniface's College to be succeeded by Brother David Kavanagh. Bishop Budd celebrated the silver jubilee of his priesthood.

1988 City Mission with final Mass at a packed Plymouth Guildhall.

1990 Fr Bartholomew Nannery from St Joseph's, Devonport, appointed cathedral administrator. Canon Bede Davis moves to Falmouth. St Therese's Court sheltered housing opens on the St Joseph's site. Bishop Christopher celebrates fourth anniversary of his consecration as bishop. Bishop Restieaux celebrates his eightieth birthday.

1991 First Gulf War. Saddam Hussein invades Kuwait.

PLYMOUTH CATHEDRAL   *Appendix*

1992 Summer catechetical camps run by the Catholic Womens' League (CWL) celebrate their fortieth anniversary.

1994 Fr Bart Nannery, the cathedral administrator, appointed a canon of the Cathedral Chapter together with Mgr George Hay (later Provost) and Fr Peter Webb.

1995 Death of Florence (Flo) Pedrick in January. Death of Canon Elwell.

1995 Cardinal Basil Hume in Plymouth on 17th May for the consecration of the new cathedral altar after three years of major re-ordering, repairs and renovation. Cardinal opens Notre Dame House sheltered housing next to the cathedral.

1995 Diocesan Assembly co-ordinating group formed as well as parish renewal teams. Publication of Assembly booklet *'Towards Our Light'*.

1996 Death of Bishop Restieaux on 26th February.

1997 First Diocesan Assembly held at Exeter University early in August with 275 delegates. Death of Canon Kennedy.

1998 Fr Philip Pedrick celebrated the diamond jubilee of his ordination.

1999 Inaugural meeting of the Diocesan Pastoral Council at Notre Dame School on 12th June.

2000 Year of Jubilee to celebrate the millennium. 150th anniversary of the formation of the Diocese of Plymouth celebrated on 23rd September with an anniversary Mass attended by Archbishop Bowen of Southwark, the Anglican bishops of Truro and Plymouth, togtether with other church leaders and civic dignitaries.

2000 Three cathedral parishioners received diocesan awards in October: Frank Tregaskis, Mary Metherell and Frank Payne, aged 96, the cathedral's oldest parishioner who had been an altar boy at the cathedral as far back as the Fourth National Catholic Congress in 1913.

2000 Retirement of Fr John Bolland, parish priest of Holy Cross, Beaumont Road, and Clergy Golfer of the Year in 1993.

2001 Canon Bartholomew Nannery created first Dean of Plymouth Cathedral. Bishop Budd awarded an honorary Life Fellowship of Newman College.

2002 Launch of Tower Fund to raise £250,000 for repairs to the cathedral spire. Bishop Christopher celebrated the ruby anniversary (40th) of his ordination at a diocesan Mass.

2002 Visit of the Papal Nuncio, Archbishop Pablo Puente, to the diocese to coincide with the 150th anniversary of the erection of the Plymouth Cathedral Chapter of canons.

2003 Death of Canon Philip Pedrick in January. Death of Barbara Tyacke, cathedral cook and housekeeper on 6th March.

2003 Silver jubilee of the election of Pope John Paul II. *Ad Limina* visit of Bishop Christopher Budd to Rome where, on 16th October, he concelebrated the Holy Father's silver jubilee Mass.

2004 Completion of restoration work on the cathedral spire. The final bill was £275,000. Sisters of Notre Dame de Namur celebrate the 200th anniversary of the founding of their Order.

2004 1250th anniversary of the martyrdom of St Boniface, patron of the cathedral celebrated all over Europe and at Crediton, the saint's birthplace as well as a special Mass at the cathedral on 30th June.

2005 Death of Pope John Paul II. Cardinal Joseph Ratzinger elected as Pope Benedict XVI on 19th April.

2006 Fiftieth edition of the *Diocesan Year Book* published by Canon Chris Smith, the diocesan archivist, who died the same year. Death of Canon Bede Davis, former cathedral administrator, in June.

2007 Parishes of the Cathedral, Holy Cross, Beaumont Road and St Joseph's, Devonport merged by canonical decree on 5th April to form one city centre parish.

2008 Plymouth Cathedral celebrates the 150th anniversary of its opening with a series of talks, concerts and events during the year and an Anniversary Mass on 22nd September in the presence of His Eminence Cardinal Cormac Murphy-O'Connor, Archbishop of Westminster, and His Excellency Archbishop Faustino Sainz Muñoz, Apostolic Nuncio to Great Britain.

Appendix
BISHOPS OF THE PLYMOUTH DIOCESE
George Errington	1851 - 1855
William Vaughan	1855 - 1902
Charles Graham	1902 - 1911
John Keily	1911 - 1928
John Barrett	1929 - 1946
Francis Grimshaw	1947 - 1954
Cyril Restieaux	1955 - 1986
Christopher Budd	1986 -

ADMINSTRATORS & DEANS OF PLYMOUTH CATHEDRAL
Herbert Woollett	1858 - 1888
William Brownlow	1888 - 1895
Thomas Courtenay	1895 - 1911
Michael Burns	1911 - 1919
Maurice Morrissy	1919 - 1923
Cyril Mahoney	1923 - 1931
Jeremiah Ryan	1932 - 1951
George Cantell	1951 - 1965
Joseph Elwell	1965 - 1980
Bede Davis	1980 - 1990
Bartholomew Nannery (Dean)	1990 -

PRIMARY SCHOOLS OF THE PARISH
The Cathedral School of St Mary
Headteacher Mrs Catherine Maltbaek, BA
Telephone: 01752 265270

St Joseph's, Chapel St, Devonport
Headteacher: Mr Brendan Gill
Telephone: 01752 563185

Holy Cross, Beaumont Road
Headteacher: Mr Paul Cotter, B Ed
Telephone: 01752 225420

PICTURE CREDITS
Where ownership is known, care has been taken to seek and obtain permission and/or licence from copyright owners. *This includes:*
The Royal Collection Picture Library
Punch Limited
The Western Morning News Co Ltd
Kitley House Hotel
Plymouth City Museum and Art Gallery
The TUC Library Collections
The Fleet Air Arm Archive
Steve Johnson (www.cyberheritage.co.uk)
Pen & Ink Publishing, Plymouth
St Boniface's College
The Sisters of Notre Dame de Namur

PLYMOUTH CATHEDRAL
The Royal British Legion
The University of Exeter
L'Osservatore Romano
...and thanks to ARTS Hotels and ARTS Cafés South West for their generous support.

MEET THE AUTHOR
In a varied career, Martin Dunning has been an outdoor pursuits instructor, child care officer, teacher, builder, stage-hand and writer. He is a native of Plymouth and has written on many local subjects: religion for *Catholic South West* and *Signpost*; outdoor pursuits for the *Western Morning News*; and local history for the *Francis Frith Book Company*, for whom he has written 17 books. He has also been a contributor to several AA walking books and the climbing magazine, *High*. Martin *(above)* lives on the shores of the Plym and, when not writing, spends most of his time hoping the weather's going to be good enough to go climbing.

... and THE EDITOR
Adrian Wardle was a chorister at Westminster Cathedral in the 1950s. He has been in publishing for forty years. He is the editor of *Catholic South West* the monthly newspaper for the diocese which he started in 1995. He also founded the Westminster Cathedral Bulletin (now *Oremus*) while on the parish council in the 1980s, and is a member of the Diocesan Editors' Forum.

... and THE RESEARCHER
Tom Healy taught economics and history at St Boniface's College for 29 years and coached Rugby football as well. In retirement, he is now Secretary of the Devon Rugby Referees' Society.

He is a parishioner of Our Lady of Mount Carmel, Efford and his daughter Kathleen was married at the cathedral in October 2007.

Index

A

African Mission, 97, 98

B

Baines, Bishop 6, 9
Barrett, Bishop John 42, 43, 44, 45, 46, 47, 52, 59, 86, 87
Bastard, Edmund 7, 12
Bishop's House 9, 16
Bishop Vaughan School 81
Boers, Fr Anthony (later, Canon) 46, 48, 49
Bourne, Cardinal 1, 46
Brien, Bernard C. 46
Brownlow, Monsignor 27
Buckfast Abbey 25, 52, 58, 61. 67
Budd, Bishop Christopher 108, 109, 110, 114, 116, 119, 120, 121, 122, 124, 127, 128, 129, 130, 131, 133

C

Cantell, Canon George 65, 69, 71, 80, 82, 92, 125, 143
Cathedral Chapter 8, 19
Cathedral School 9
Catholic Emancipation Act 5
Catholic Young Men's Society 32
Christ the King Church 77, 78, 89
Civil War (English) 1
Clifford, Fr. William (later Canon and Bishop) 8, 19, 26

Clifford, Lord 38
Cliffords of Chudleigh 2, 11
Congress, National Catholic 1913 7, 11, 32, 33

D

Dartmoor Prison 3, 29, 54
Dartmouth 3
Davis, Fr Bede (later Canon) 84, 91, 103, 113, 136
Dublin, Easter Rising 35, 36

E

Elizabeth I, Queen 1
Elwell, Canon Joseph 90, 92, 103, 124
English Gothic 12
English Hierarchy 7
Errington, Bishop George 7, 8, 12, 19, 24, 26, 76
Exeter 2
Exeter, Bishop of 2, 26

F

Flynn, Fr Thomas 3
Ford Park Cemetery 9

G

Gaynor, Canon Walter 36, 70
Graham, Canon Charles (later Bishop) 13, 17, 27
Griffin, Cardinal Bernard 65, 66
Grimshaw, Bishop Francis 63, 64, 65, 66, 67, 68, 71, 80

Guilbert, Abbé Louis 4

H

Hansom Brothers, Charles & Joseph 12, 13, 14, 16
Hawker, Rev. Robert 4
Hawker, Rev. Robert Vicar of Morwenstow 23
Henry VIII, King 1
Heenan, Cardinal John 88
HMS Hotspur, Catholic Chapel 9
Holy Redeemer Church 57, 64, 65, 130
Hospital, Royal Naval 4, 35
Hume, Cardinal Basil 93, 94, 101, 104, 109, 118, 119, 120

I

Irish Catholics 3, 23
Irish Christian Brothers 45
Irish Famine 22
'Irish Question' 22, 34

J

James II, King 2

K

Keily, Bishop John 23, 31, 32, 33, 34, 40, 41, 42, 44, 63

L

Leopold-de-Prins 14
List of Papists 2
Little Sisters of the Poor 5, 79

Appendix

M
Mahoney, Canon 36
Manning, Cardinal 23
Mc Auliffe Dr 12
Mc Donnell, Fr Thomas 5, 7
Murphy-O'Connor, Cardinal Cormac 101

N
Nannery, Canon (Fr) Bartholomew 20, 103, 106, 111, 112, 113, 116, 118, 119, 121, 122, 128, 130, 132, 135
Notre Dame, Sisters of, 4, 24, 25, 26, 45, 53, 55, 58, 76, 81, 115, 135

O
Oliver, Dr George (Provost) 19

P
Pedrick family 84, 85, 109, 124
Pike, Winifred Mary 142
Plymouth Dock (later Devonport) 2
Poor Sisters of Nazareth 45
Pope Gregory XVI 6
Pope John Paul II 95, 113, 133
Pope Pius IX 6
Pope Pius XI 40, 41, 48, 49

R
Redemptorist Fathers 71
Restieaux, Bishop Cyril 69, 71, 72, 73, 77, 83, 84, 85, 87, 88, 91, 93, 94, 95, 99, 100, 101, 102, 104, 106, 108, 109, 111, 114, 122, 123

Riley, Fr Henry 5
Roberts, Mr (builder) 12
Royal Theatre (Foulston's) 14
Ryan, Canon Jeremiah 54, 65, 71, 82, 89

S
Sabbath Day Fight 1
Secular Clergy Fund 9
Sheehan, Canon Patrick 29
Sisters of St Anne 46, 86, 104
Spithead Mutiny 3
St Boniface Centenary Congress 67, 68, 73
St Boniface's College 58, 61, 76, 88, 95, 105, 110
St Cuthbert Mayne 87, 93
St Martin-in-the-Fields 19
St Mary's Chapel 4, 5, 9
SS Michael & Joseph Church (Devonport) 24, 106, 111, 112

T
Te Deum 1
Timmings, Fr Charles 3
Trelawney, Miss Ann Letitia 4, 141
Trelawney, Sir Harry 141, 142
Turner, Fr Christopher 2

V
Vatican Council, First 140
Vatican Council, Second 83, 95, 100, 145
Vaughan, Bishop William 8, 11, 12, 13, 15, 16, 17, 18, 21, 22, 23, 25, 26, 27, 28, 29, 106, 136

PLYMOUTH CATHEDRAL

Victoria, Queen 6
Vonier, Fr Anscar Abbot of Buckfast 44

W
Walmsley, Bishop 3
Walmsley, Bishop Military Vicariate 97
William of Orange, King 2
Williams, Fr Edward 2
Wiseman, Cardinal Nicholas 6, 8, 11
Woollett, Canon Herbert 9, 15, 16, 19, 23, 26

Compiled by
Tom Healy

This statue of Our Lady and the infant Jesus dominates the Lady Chapel at the east end of the cathedral.

The Blessed Sacrament Chapel.